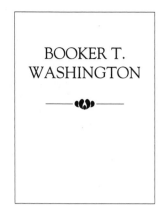

BOOKER T.
WASHINGTON

BOOKER T. WASHINGTON

Alan Schroeder

Senior Consulting Editor
Nathan Irvin Huggins
Director
W.E.B. Du Bois Institute for Afro-American Research
Harvard University

CHELSEA HOUSE PUBLISHERS
New York   Philadelphia

To my good friend Nicola ("Nikki") King —A. S.

Chelsea House Publishers
Editor-in-Chief Remmel Nunn
Managing Editor Karyn Gullen Browne
Copy Chief Mark Rifkin
Picture Editor Adrian G. Allen
Art Director Maria Epes
Assistant Art Director Howard Brotman
Manufacturing Director Gerald Levine
Systems Manager Lindsey Ottman
Production Manager Joseph Romano
Production Coordinator Marie Claire Cebrián

Black Americans of Achievement
Senior Editor Richard Rennert

Staff for BOOKER T. WASHINGTON
Copy Editor Christopher Duffy
Editorial Assistant Michele Berezansky
Designer Ghila Krajzman
Picture Researchers Alan Gottlieb, Jennifer Stevens
Cover Illustration Bill Donahey

First Printing

1 3 5 7 9 8 6 4 2

Library of Congress Cataloging-in-Publication Data
Schroeder, Alan.
    Booker T. Washington, educator and racial spokesman/by Alan
Schroeder.
    p. cm.—(Black Americans of achievement)
    Includes bibliographical references and index.
    ISBN   1-55546-616-8
           0-7910-0252-7 (pbk.)
1. Washington, Booker T., 1856–1915—Juvenile literature. 2. Afro-
Americans—Biography—Juvenile literature. 3. Educators—United
States—Biography— Juvenile literature. I. Title. II. Series.
E185.97.W4S24 1992   91-25416
378.1'11—dc20   CIP
[B]   AC

Frontispiece:
*Booker T. Washington, America's
leading black spokesman in the late
19th and early 20th centuries, in his
office at Tuskegee Institute.*

CONTENTS

BLACK AMERICANS OF ACHIEVEMENT

HANK AARON
baseball great

KAREEM ABDUL-JABBAR
basketball great

RALPH ABERNATHY
civil rights leader

ALVIN AILEY
choreographer

MUHAMMAD ALI
heavyweight champion

RICHARD ALLEN
religious leader and social activist

MAYA ANGELOU
author

LOUIS ARMSTRONG
musician

ARTHUR ASHE
tennis great

JOSEPHINE BAKER
entertainer

JAMES BALDWIN
author

BENJAMIN BANNEKER
scientist and mathematician

AMIRI BARAKA
poet and playwright

COUNT BASIE
bandleader and composer

ROMARE BEARDEN
artist

JAMES BECKWOURTH
frontiersman

MARY McLEOD BETHUNE
educator

JULIAN BOND
civil rights leader and politician

GWENDOLYN BROOKS
poet

JIM BROWN
football great

BLANCHE BRUCE
politician

RALPH BUNCHE
diplomat

STOKELY CARMICHAEL
civil rights leader

GEORGE WASHINGTON CARVER
botanist

RAY CHARLES
musician

CHARLES CHESNUTT
author

JOHN COLTRANE
musician

BILL COSBY
entertainer

PAUL CUFFE
merchant and abolitionist

COUNTEE CULLEN
poet

ANGELA DAVIS
civil rights leader

BENJAMIN DAVIS, SR., AND BENJAMIN DAVIS, JR.
military leaders

SAMMY DAVIS, JR.
entertainter

FATHER DIVINE
religious leader

FREDERICK DOUGLASS
abolitionist editor

CHARLES DREW
physician

W.E.B. DU BOIS
scholar and activist

PAUL LAURENCE DUNBAR
poet

KATHERINE DUNHAM
dancer and choreographer

DUKE ELLINGTON
bandleader and composer

RALPH ELLISON
author

JULIUS ERVING
basketball great

JAMES FARMER
civil rights leader

ELLA FITZGERALD
singer

MARCUS GARVEY
black nationalist leader

JOSH GIBSON
baseball great

DIZZY GILLESPIE
musician

CLARA McBRIDE ("MOTHER") HALE
humanitarian

PRINCE HALL
social reformer

W. C. HANDY
father of the blues

WILLIAM HASTIE
educator and politician

MATTHEW HENSON
explorer

CHESTER HIMES
author

BILLIE HOLIDAY
singer

JOHN HOPE
educator

LENA HORNE
entertainer

LANGSTON HUGHES
poet

ZORA NEALE HURSTON
author

JESSE JACKSON
civil rights leader and politician

MICHAEL JACKSON
entertainer

JACK JOHNSON
heavyweight champion

JAMES WELDON JOHNSON
author

SCOTT JOPLIN
composer

BARBARA JORDAN
politician

CORETTA SCOTT KING
civil rights leader

MARTIN LUTHER KING, JR.
civil rights leader

SPIKE LEE
filmmaker

REGINALD LEWIS
entrepreneur

ALAIN LOCKE
scholar and educator

JOE LOUIS
heavyweight champion

RONALD MCNAIR
astronaut

MALCOLM X
militant black leader

THURGOOD MARSHALL
Supreme Court justice

TONI MORRISON
author

CONSTANCE BAKER MOTLEY
civil rights leader and judge

ELIJAH MUHAMMAD
religious leader

EDDIE MURPHY
entertainer

JESSE OWENS
champion athlete

SATCHEL PAIGE
baseball great

CHARLIE PARKER
musician

GORDON PARKS
photographer

ROSA PARKS
civil rights leader

SIDNEY POITIER
actor

ADAM CLAYTON
POWELL, JR.
political leader

COLIN POWELL
military leader

LEONTYNE PRICE
opera singer

A. PHILIP RANDOLPH
labor leader

PAUL ROBESON
singer and actor

JACKIE ROBINSON
baseball great

DIANA ROSS
entertainer

BILL RUSSELL
basketball great

JOHN RUSSWURM
publisher

SOJOURNER TRUTH
antislavery activist

HARRIET TUBMAN
antislavery activist

NAT TURNER
slave revolt leader

DENMARK VESEY
slave revolt leader

ALICE WALKER
author

MADAM C. J. WALKER
entrepreneur

BOOKER T. WASHINGTON
educator and racial spokesman

IDA WELLS-BARNETT
civil rights leader

WALTER WHITE
civil rights leader

OPRAH WINFREY
entertainer

STEVIE WONDER
musician

RICHARD WRIGHT
author

ON ACHIEVEMENT

Coretta Scott King

BEFORE YOU BEGIN this book, I hope you will ask yourself what the word *excellence* means to you. I think that it's a question we should all ask, and keep asking as we grow older and change. Because the truest answer to it should never change. When you think of excellence, perhaps you think of success at work; or of becoming wealthy; or meeting the right person, getting married, and having a good family life.

Those important goals are worth striving for, but there is a better way to look at excellence. As Martin Luther King, Jr., said in one of his last sermons, "I want you to be first in love. I want you to be first in moral excellence. I want you to be first in generosity. If you want to be important, wonderful. If you want to be great, wonderful. But recognize that he who is greatest among you shall be your servant."

My husband, Martin Luther King, Jr., knew that the true meaning of achievement is service. When I met him, in 1952, he was already ordained as a Baptist preacher and was working toward a doctoral degree at Boston University. I was studying at the New England Conservatory and dreamed of accomplishments in music. We married a year later, and after I graduated the following year we moved to Montgomery, Alabama. We didn't know it then, but our notions of achievement were about to undergo a dramatic change.

You may have read or heard about what happened next. What began with the boycott of a local bus line grew into a national movement, and by the time he was assassinated in 1968 my husband had fashioned a black movement powerful enough to shatter forever the practice of racial segregation. What you may not have read about is where he got his method for resisting injustice without compromising his religious beliefs.

He adopted the strategy of nonviolence from a man of a different race, who lived in a different country, and even practiced a different religion. The man was Mahatma Gandhi, the great leader of India, who devoted his life to serving humanity in the spirit of love and nonviolence. It was in these principles that Martin discovered his method for social reform. More than anything else, those two principles were the key to his achievements.

This book is about black Americans who served society through the excellence of their achievements. It forms a part of the rich history of black men and women in America—a history of stunning accomplishments in every field of human endeavor, from literature and art to science, industry, education, diplomacy, athletics, jurisprudence, even polar exploration.

Not all of the people in this history had the same ideals, but I think you will find something that all of them had in common. Like Martin Luther King, Jr., they all decided to become "drum majors" and serve humanity. In that principle—whether it was expressed in books, inventions, or song—they found something outside themselves to use as a goal and a guide. Something that showed them a way to serve others, instead of only living for themselves.

Reading the stories of these courageous men and women not only helps us discover the principles that we will use to guide our own lives but also teaches us about our black heritage and about America itself. It is crucial for us to know the heroes and heroines of our history and to realize that the price we paid in our struggle for equality in America was dear. But we must also understand that we have gotten as far as we have partly because America's democratic system and ideals made it possible.

We are still struggling with racism and prejudice. But the great men and women in this series are a tribute to the spirit of our democratic ideals and the system in which they have flourished. And that makes their stories special and worth knowing.

1

ATLANTA, 1895

O N THE MORNING of September 18, 1895, Booker T. Washington arose early in an Atlanta, Georgia, boardinghouse and began to dress. He had slept poorly the night before, and as he buttoned his shirt, his fingers trembled slightly. After he had combed his hair and adjusted his tie, he picked up a handwritten sheet of paper and began to study it quietly. The paper contained the speech he was scheduled to give that afternoon at the opening of the Cotton States and International Exposition.

Washington knew the words by heart; nevertheless, he read them again, trying in his mind to hear them for the first time. He understood that his speech had to be absolutely right. He could not afford to make a bad impression at the opening ceremony of the exposition. There would be many whites in the audience who would enjoy watching a black man make a fool of himself in front of thousands of people. Washington was determined not to let that happen.

Booker T. Washington exhorts a gathering of blacks in Louisiana to gain a foothold in their nation's economy before they attempt to seek political and social equality. This accommodationist approach to racial progress helped establish him as the most powerful black American of his time.

The grounds of the 1895 Cotton States and International Exposition in Atlanta, Georgia, where Washington gave the Atlanta Compromise, the landmark speech that earned him the title of the Great Accommodator. The 39-year-old educator said in the address that blacks should concentrate on education and economic growth rather than pursue "the extremest folly" of agitating for civil rights.

After studying his speech, the 39-year-old educator knelt and said a short prayer, as he always did before making any public address.

An hour or so later, a committee of distinguished black men arrived at the boardinghouse to escort Washington and his family to the exposition. Hundreds of gaily decorated carriages and wagons jammed the streets of Atlanta. The heat that morning was intense, and during the long and bumpy ride, Washington must have wondered how much controversy his presence at the opening-day ceremony would cause. "It was only a few years before that time," he later wrote, "that any white man in the audience might have claimed me as his slave. . . . I knew, too, that this was the first time . . . that a member of my race had been asked to speak from the same platform with white Southern men and women on any important National occasion."

The dirt road became so crowded with horses and pedestrians that it took three hours for Washington's carriage to arrive at the exposition. "When we reached the grounds," he remembered, "the heat, together with my nervous anxiety, made me feel as if I were about ready to collapse, and to feel that my address was not going to be a success." With his wife and children in tow, Washington squeezed his way through the crowd until he reached the main building where the opening remarks were to be delivered. The auditorium, he discovered, was packed from top to bottom; thousands of people milled outside, unable to get in.

By early afternoon, it was time for the exposition to officially begin. With appropriate pomp, "The Star-Spangled Banner" was played, immediately followed by "Dixie," the rousing anthem of the South. As the dignitaries filed onstage, the crowd began to cheer loudly. Washington was one of the last men to enter. As soon as he became visible, the white members of the audience abruptly ceased their cheering and shouting. Bewildered voices filled the auditorium. An angry man could be heard above the din: "What's that nigger doing on the stage?"

Washington did his best to hide his embarrassment. He took his seat with the others, folded his hands on his lap, and waited patiently through a long series of invocations and opening remarks. The air in the auditorium was stifling. After a while, the audience began to grow restless as the dignitaries droned on.

Looking out at the crowd, Washington knew that for his speech to succeed, it would have to appeal to a broad cross section of people: white northerners, white southerners, and blacks. This would not be easy. For weeks, he had diligently worked on his address, reading aloud the various drafts to his wife Maggie and the faculty at his black school in Tuskegee, Alabama. To his relief, everyone had seemed pleased with the final version.

At last, it was Washington's turn to speak. He was graciously introduced by former Georgia governor Rufus Bullock: "We shall now be favored with an address by a great Southern educator." The fatigued members of the audience began to applaud. Washington rose from his seat and made his way to the front of the stage. Instantly, the applause died. No one in the auditorium could believe that the "great Southern educator" was black. Washington faced the crowd nervously. He knew that he had reached a critical moment in his career.

His first words were appropriately benign. He reminded his listeners that one-third of the southern population was black and that never before had the value "of the American Negro been more fittingly and generously recognized than by the managers of this magnificent Exposition. . . . It is a recognition that will do more to cement the friendship of the two races than any occurrence since the dawn of our freedom."

So far, so good. The white members of the audience—their anger thus defused—settled back to hear what the black educator had to say. In a quiet but firm voice, Washington encouraged southern blacks to make every effort to get along with their white neighbors. Economically and politically, he said, their interests were the same. For the common good of the South, they should join hands "in agriculture, mechanics, in commerce, in domestic service, and in the professions."

At the same time, Washington reminded blacks to become educated. Until the race could read and write, the majority of southern blacks would have to earn their living as common laborers. This, on the other hand, was no cause for shame. In Washington's opinion, any black man who considered himself too good for manual labor was a stiff-necked fool.

"No race can prosper," he told the crowd, "till it learns that there is as much dignity in tilling a field as in writing a poem. It is at the bottom of life we must begin, and not at the top." This last remark especially pleased the white members of the audience, who by this time were paying close attention. They, too, believed that blacks should start at the bottom. (Unfortunately, they also believed that blacks should stay there.)

Washington had words of advice for the whites as well. He reminded them to help and encourage southern blacks, "the most patient, faithful, law-abiding, and unresentful people that the world has seen." At this point, Washington's speech waxed sentimental: "As we have proved our loyalty to you in the past, in nursing your children, watching by the

Exhibits at the 1895 Cotton States and International Exposition were meant to encourage white northerners to invest in southern industry. Washington, who had been asked to present the Negro Exhibit, did his part to attract northern investment by promising increased cooperation between southern blacks and whites.

sick-bed of your mothers and fathers, and often following them with tear-dimmed eyes to their graves, so in the future, in our humble way, we shall stand by you . . . ready to lay down our lives, if need be, in defence of yours, interlacing our industrial, commercial, civil, and religious life with yours in a way that shall make the interests of both races one." The southern portion of the audience was deeply moved, and Washington's words were interrupted by a spontaneous outburst of applause.

The sunlight, meanwhile, was shining directly into Washington's eyes, but he continued to stare straight ahead. "The sinews stood out on his bronzed neck," a reporter later wrote, "and his muscular right arm swung high in the air with a lead pencil grasped in the clenched brown fist."

Washington went on to say that any effort made by whites to advance the black race would be amply rewarded. "We shall constitute one-third and more of the ignorance and crime of the South," he warned, "or one-third its intelligence and progress; we shall contribute one-third to the business and industrial prosperity of the South, or we shall prove a veritable body of death, stagnating, depressing, retarding every effort to advance the body politic." Again, Washington warmly thanked everyone present for already having done so much to educate the southern black population—especially "Northern philanthropists, who have made their gifts a constant stream of blessing and encouragement."

As he neared the end of his speech, Washington touched upon the sensitive issue of black civil rights. It would be "the extremest folly," he said, for blacks to agitate for social equality at the present time. Taking this idea one step further, Washington made it clear that he believed civil rights for blacks should be earned and not simply given. "It is important and right that all privileges of the law be ours," he said, "but it is vastly more important that we be prepared for the exercises of these privileges."

In essence, Washington was telling southern blacks to be patient, to put aside the question of civil rights temporarily, and to concentrate instead on education and other forms of self-improvement. This was a program for racial progress that southern whites could fully support, and the moment Washington finished his speech, the audience rose to its feet, cheering and shouting. According to one account, "Handkerchiefs were waved, canes were flourished, hats were tossed in the air. The fairest women of Georgia stood and cheered." Bullock, a former slave owner, rushed across the stage and began to pump Washington's hand enthusiastically. "I received so many and such hearty congratulations," Washington remembered, "that I found it difficult to get out of the building."

Two days later, he returned with his family to his home in Tuskegee. By this time, the effects of Washington's speech had reverberated across the nation; everywhere, people were discussing the Atlanta Compromise. No longer was Booker T. Washington an obscure southern educator. Overnight, he had become the most celebrated and respected black American of his generation. 〰

2

A CHILD OF SLAVERY

$\mathbf{A}$CCORDING TO A family Bible, which has since been lost, Booker T. Washington was born a slave in the state of Virginia on April 5, 1856. From the moment of his birth, he was the legal property of James Burroughs, a respectable landowner who got along well with his slaves.

For the first 9 years of his life, Booker lived with his mother and siblings in a squalid cabin on Burroughs's 207-acre farm. The "plantation," as Booker called it, was located near the village of Hale's Ford, in the rolling hills of northeast Franklin County, at the foot of the Blue Ridge Mountains.

Booker's mother, a slave named Jane, was the plantation's cook. The identity of his father remains uncertain. "Whoever he was," Booker wrote, "I never heard of his taking the least interest in me or providing in any way for my rearing." Like his elder brother, John, Booker was a mulatto baby, with medium brown skin, grey eyes, full lips, and reddish hair. His father was almost certainly a white man, possibly the son of a neighboring landowner or a field hand.

A view of the log cabin on the Burroughs plantation near Hale's Ford, Virginia, where Washington was born. The estate, which has since been restored to reflect its appearance and operation during his early life as a slave, is now a national monument.

A stone's throw from the log cabin where Washington was born and raised was the house in which his owners, the Burroughses, resided. "When I had grown to sufficient size," he recalled, "I was required to go to the 'big house' at meal-times to fan the flies from the table."

Around 1860, when she was 40, Booker's mother married Washington Ferguson, a 51-year-old slave from a neighboring plantation. By necessity, the marriage was informal. Ferguson's master was a cruel man, and only on rare occasions was Ferguson able to slip across the road to visit his wife. It was not until after the Civil War that Booker came to know his stepfather well.

When they were not laboring in the fields, the half-dozen slaves on the Burroughs estate were confined to two log cabins and a tiny yard overgrown with weeds. A stone's throw from the slave quarters stood the "big house," where 62-year-old James Burroughs lived with his wife, Elizabeth, and their 14 children (half of whom had moved away by 1856, the year Booker was born).

James Burroughs was a man of neither wealth nor influence. He was a self-sufficient farmer living from one season to the next. Tobacco was his primary crop, but he grew other things as well, including wheat, corn, oats, flax, and sweet potatoes. Like many white southerners, Burroughs and his sons found it necessary to work side by side with their slaves in the corn and wheat fields. "In this way," Booker recalled, "we all grew up together, very much like members of one big family."

Naturally, Booker and the other slaves did not eat as well or live as comfortably as the master and his children. The dismal cabin where Jane and her family lived was cramped and filthy. In the center of the dirt floor, there was a deep pit, covered with boards, where sweet potatoes were stored during the winter. The cabin door—"that is," Booker recalled, "something that was called a door"—hung dejectedly on rusty hinges. Gaping holes in the walls served as windows. There was hardly any furniture and no stove.

All year long, Jane sweated in front of the open fireplace, cooking 3 meals a day for 20 hungry people.

In July and August, the heat in the cabin was overpowering, and Booker spent most of his time outside in the yard, playing marbles and hide-and-seek with his brother, John, and his younger sister, Amanda.

At night, after the fire had been extinguished, the family slept on three or four grain sacks strewn across the dirt floor. There were no beds in the slave cabins; such luxuries were reserved for the master and his family. Booker was 10 years old before he slept in a bed for the first time.

Food was scarce in the slave quarters, and according to Booker, he took his meals where he could find them. Sometimes, when no one was looking, he would snatch a sweet potato from the hole in the dirt floor. Other days, he would eat the boiled corn that was supposed to have been fed to the hogs. One evening, in fearful silence, the family cooked and ate a chicken, which Jane had somehow managed to steal from the barnyard.

Because she was constantly busy with her cooking, Jane was not able to give much attention to her young children. As toddlers, Booker and John spent much of their time sitting in the yard, watching the other slaves go about their chores. As soon as their fingers were strong enough to grip a hoe, however, they were put to work feeding the hogs and toting pails of water to the men in the fields.

It was around this time that Booker first became aware of his desire to learn. Education in the South, even among the upper classes, was not considered a high priority. The school year lasted less than four months, attendance was spotty, and too often the instructors themselves were poorly educated. Nevertheless, James Burroughs sent his daughters to the local schoolhouse to learn what they could. Booker was occasionally told to follow behind the girls and carry their books for them. He did not mind doing

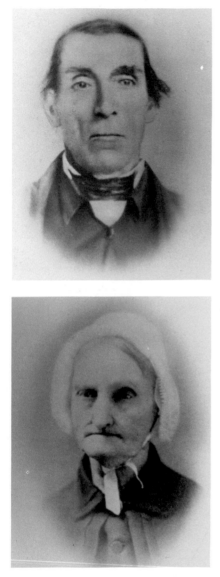

"My owners were not especially cruel," Washington said of James Burroughs (top) and his wife, Elizabeth (bottom). Nevertheless, young Booker was forced to spend almost every day "occupied in some kind of labour."

this because it gave him an opportunity to peek into the small schoolhouse, where he saw rows of white children obediently reciting the alphabet and reading aloud from their primers. This sight, he recalled, "made a deep impression upon me, and I had the feeling that to get into a schoolhouse and study in this way would be about the same as getting into paradise."

In the South, however, it was illegal to teach a slave how to read and write, and it is unlikely that anyone would have encouraged Booker's educational dream. His mother made a point of telling him that reading was a "dangerous" business only meant for white folks. The word *dangerous* fascinated Booker, and he resolved that someday he would learn to read and write, even if he had to teach himself how.

In general, life in Franklin County was slow and uneventful. There were no large cities nearby, and the monotony was broken only by an occasional lawsuit or a runaway horse or the appearance of a public speaker. Most people went around barefoot; men chewed tobacco, and it was not unusual for women to smoke corncob pipes and dip snuff.

The tranquillity of this rural life was shattered, however, by the outbreak of the Civil War, which swiftly became the bloodiest conflict in the nation's history. The first shots were fired in South Carolina on April 12, 1861, when Booker was five years old. By the end of April, a total of 11 southern states, including Virginia, had seceded from the Union. Though many factors were involved, the war was being fought primarily over the controversial issue of slavery: The North wanted to abolish it, and the South, for social and economic reasons, wished to preserve it.

Everyone in Franklin County followed the events of the war closely. Only a handful of blacks were able to read the newspapers, but there was an effective oral network called the "grapevine telegraph" that kept everyone informed. News passed from kitchen to kitchen, and field to field, with surprising speed. "Often," Booker recalled, "the slaves got knowledge of the results of great battles before the white people received it."

Booker's master, James Burroughs, died in July 1861, three months after the start of the war. By this time, Booker and his brother were considered old enough and strong enough to take on some of the heavier chores around the farm. According to Booker, one of his weekly duties was to take the corn to the mill to be ground. "This work I always dreaded," he later wrote. "The heavy bag of corn would be thrown across the back of the horse, and the corn divided about evenly on each side." During the three-mile journey to the mill, however, the grain would usually shift weight, causing the bag to tumble to the ground. Booker was not strong enough to pick up the load, so he had no choice but to sit by the roadside, in tears, waiting for someone to come along and lend a hand.

Returning home from the mill was even more traumatic. Along the way, Booker had to pass through a dense and shadowy forest. "I was always frightened," he remembered. "The woods were said to be full of soldiers who had deserted from the army, and I had been told that the first thing a deserter did to a Negro boy when he found him alone was to cut off his ears."

By the summer of 1862, more than 100,000 Americans had been killed or wounded in the Civil War. Deeply grieved by the ongoing conflict, President Abraham Lincoln drafted a sweeping measure that he hoped would cripple the South's economy and eventually bring the fighting to an end. On September 22, 1862, with the approval of his cabinet, Lincoln issued the Emancipation Proclamation. This important piece of legislation declared that, as of January 1, 1863, all slaves living in the Confederate South were to "be then, thenceforward, and forever

A Union soldier informs a group of slaves that the Emancipation Proclamation, issued by President Abraham Lincoln in September 1862, has declared them "forever free." Washington witnessed a similar scene at the conclusion of the Civil War, when a U.S. government official rode up to the Burroughs plantation and read an announcement to young Booker and his family stating they were no longer slaves.

Students and their teachers assemble in front of a Franklin County, Virginia, schoolhouse near the Burroughs plantation. Even though it was illegal for a slave to be taught to read and write, Washington resolved to learn those skills after escorting his owners' daughters to school and observing a classroom filled with white children reading from their primers.

free." In theory, this proclamation liberated millions of blacks who had spent their life in bondage. The majority of southern whites, however, did not recognize the legality of Lincoln's order, and slavery continued to flourish.

Two years later, in September 1864, the city of Atlanta, Georgia, was invaded by Union troops led by General William T. Sherman. After torching Atlanta, Sherman's men began to march victoriously toward Savannah, leaving behind them a bloody wake of death and destruction. Everywhere, Southerners were thrown into a state of panic and confusion. Banks and businesses closed; cities were evacuated; food prices tripled, then quadrupled. Armed groups of white men patrolled the roads, searching for runaway slaves. Despite the increased surveillance, Booker's stepfather, Washington Ferguson, managed to escape his master's tyranny, slipping across the border into the new state of West Virginia to live as a free man.

Meanwhile, three and a half million slaves hoped and prayed for the defeat of the Confederate army. "As the great day drew nearer," Booker recalled, "there was more singing in the slave quarters than usual. It was bolder, had more ring, and lasted later into the night."

In April 1865, the Union army seized the Confederate capital of Richmond, Virginia. This was a
crushing blow to the Southerners, and a week later,
on April 9, the Confederate commander, Robert E.
Lee, formally surrendered to the commander of the
Union army, Ulysses S. Grant. To the relief of the
shattered nation, the Civil War had at last come to
an end.

A day or two after Lee's surrender, a government
official rode up to the veranda of the Burroughs home.
Before the assembled group of masters and slaves, he
made a short speech, then began to read from a sheet
of paper, presumably the Emancipation Proclamation. "After the reading," Booker remembered, "we
were told that we were all free, and could go when
and where we pleased. My mother, who was standing
by my side, leaned over and kissed her children, while
tears of joy ran down her cheeks. . . . For some minutes
there was great rejoicing, and thanksgiving, and wild
scenes of ecstasy."

After the initial jubilation had worn off, however,
a strange feeling of seriousness, even gloom, began to
descend upon the former slaves. A new and somewhat
disturbing thought had occurred to them. Financially,
they were now responsible for themselves. They could
no longer rely on their masters for food and shelter.
As free people, they had to find their place in society.

According to Booker, "It was very much like
suddenly turning a youth of ten or twelve years out
into the world to provide for himself. . . . Some of
the slaves were seventy or eighty years old; their best
days were gone. They had no strength with which to
earn a living in a strange place and among strange
people. . . . Gradually, one by one, stealthily at first,
the older slaves began to wander from the slave
quarters back to the 'big house' to have a whispered
conversation with their former owners as to their
future." ❧

3

THE DESIRE TO LEARN

DURING THE WEEKS that followed the conclusion of the Civil War, many former slaves (or freedmen, as they were called) temporarily left their plantations and farms. It was important for them to feel that they could come and go as they pleased—to "try their freedom on," as Booker T. Washington called it.

Many returned after a day or two, bewildered by the prospect of having to find new employment. The majority of freedmen were illiterate and therefore unable to compete in the urban marketplace. For many, it was easiest to work out some sort of arrangement with their former master that would allow them to stay on the plantation. There was safety and comfort in familiarity.

Booker's stepfather was more fortunate than most. After escaping to the state of West Virginia in 1864, Washington Ferguson had managed to find work as a salt packer in the small town of Malden. By 1865, he had saved some money, and after the war, he wrote (or had someone write) to his wife, telling her to join him there. Jane and the children promptly loaded

Washington lived in this cabin after moving with his mother, Jane; brother, John; sister, Amanda; and stepfather, Washington Ferguson, to Malden, West Virginia, in 1865. Even though they were no longer slaves, Booker recalled that "our new house was no better than the one we had left on the old plantation in Virginia."

their few possessions into a wagon, and after bidding farewell to the Burroughs family, they began their journey west. Because Jane's health was beginning to fail, she rode in the wagon; the three children followed behind on foot.

Two weeks later, exhausted but optimistic, they arrived in Malden, a river town eight miles from Charleston. As they made their way up the main street, they must have been discouraged by what they saw. The neighborhood where Washington Ferguson lived was crowded and filthy; the smell of rotting garbage and animal dung permeated the air. Poor blacks and poor whites lived side by side in mutual squalor. According to Booker, "Drinking, gambling, quarrels, fights, and shockingly immoral practices were frequent."

The cabin where the family lived was just as small and uncomfortable as the one on the Burroughs farm. It was also twice as dirty. For obvious reasons, nine-year-old Booker took an immediate dislike to the community of Malden.

Within a matter of days, he and John were put to work at the salt furnace where their stepfather earned wages as a packer. All day long, the boys shoveled dried salt into large wooden barrels, pounding down the loose salt until each barrel weighed a standard amount. The job was backbreaking, and Washington Ferguson pocketed what little money his stepsons earned.

At the end of each day, the salt barrels were numbered according to who had done the packing. The Fergusons' number was 18. A bright boy, Booker quickly learned what the number 18 looked like, drawing it in the dirt with a stick. In time, he probably began to recognize other numbers as well. The letters of the alphabet, however, remained a mystery to him.

Like many freedmen, Booker had a burning desire to read and write. Working every day at the salt

furnace, though, allowed him no time to pursue an education. The salt packers began work at dawn, and they never left the furnace before dusk. In addition to this, packing salt was hard and heavy work, and every night when Booker returned home, he felt exhausted. Nevertheless, he understood that he *had* to become educated. It was the only means by which he could escape his life of drudgery.

One evening, to Booker's surprise, his mother presented him with a copy of a *Webster's* spelling book. From then on, whenever he was at home, Booker could be found studying the alphabet, putting letters together, forming words and simple sentences. In this crude way, without any assistance, he managed to teach himself most of the alphabet.

His determination to learn was not unusual. During the postwar period known as Reconstruction, an increasingly large number of freedmen began to seek an education. They believed that if they could learn to read and write, they could get better jobs,

A familiar sight to Washington during his early adolescence: a salt mine along the Kanawha River. "Salt-mining was the great industry in that part of West Virginia," he said of the Kanawha Valley, where he lived from 1865 to 1872, "and the little town of Malden was right in the midst of the salt-furnaces. . . . Though I was a mere child, my stepfather put me and my brother at work in one of the furnaces. Often I began work as early as four o'clock in the morning."

begin to buy property, and eventually win the right to vote. As Booker later put it, "A whole race [was] beginning to go to school for the first time. . . . Few were too young, and none too old, to make the attempt to learn. . . . Day-school, night-school, Sunday-school, were always crowded, and often many had to be turned away for want of room."

Not long after Booker's arrival in West Virginia, a black school was established in the nearby community of Tinkersville, one mile from Malden. The school excited a great deal of interest; according to Booker, it was the first of its kind in the area. His stepfather, however, would not let him attend. Booker was told that every dime he earned as a packer was needed to put food on the table. This was probably true, and yet it was during this supposedly lean period that Booker's parents decided to adopt a fourth child, an orphan boy whom they named James B. Washington.

Naturally, Booker was discouraged by his stepfather's decision, but he refused to give up his goal of acquiring an education. As soon as it could be arranged, he began to attend night school, an experience he found to be so rewarding "that I think I learned more at night than the other children did during the day."

The first evening that Booker attended the Tinkersville school, he was asked to recite his name. This request perplexed him. As a slave child, he had never been called anything but Booker. He had no idea what his full name was or if he even had one. Perhaps thinking of his stepfather, the name Booker Washington sprang to his lips, and this was what he called himself for the next few years. Later, when Booker was a teenager, his mother told him that his middle name was Taliaferro (pronounced Tol-uh-ver). Only then, when he was about 16, did he begin to call himself Booker T. Washington.

After a while, when it became clear that Booker was serious about pursuing his education, his stepfather changed his mind, and together they worked out an arrangement that permitted Booker to attend school during the day. "I was to rise early in the morning," Booker remembered, "and work in the furnace till nine o'clock, and return immediately after school closed in the afternoon for at least two more hours of work." This proved to be a grueling schedule, however, and after a month or two, Booker returned to night school.

Like most black schools in the South, the one in Tinkersville was very small. Until suitable quarters could be found, classes were held in the bedroom of a local home. The teacher was a young educated black man, a Civil War veteran named William Davis. Charismatic and extremely conscientious, Davis was largely responsible for the school's success. Within 2 years, attendance had risen from approximately 30 to 79 students.

Initially, the school received no funding from the state or county. Each black family, therefore, was asked to contribute a small amount of money to pay for books and supplies. It was also agreed that the teacher, William Davis, could "board 'round," living with a different family each day of the month. Booker always looked forward to the evening when his family could entertain the learned Mr. Davis.

Eventually, the county began to set aside funds for the Tinkersville school—but such allocations were usually small and grudgingly given. According to one principal in nearby Charleston, the local school board was made up of "ignorant, coarse-minded men" who could not see the necessity of providing desks in black classrooms. The situation in Tinkersville was no better. "General apathy prevails," stated William Davis, "where there is not decided prejudice and opposition."

"I determined, when quite a small child," Washington said, "that, if I accomplished nothing else in life, I would in some way get enough education to enable me to read common books and newspapers." William Davis, who headed a black school in Tinkersville, West Virginia, and served as Booker's first teacher, was among the people who helped him realize his goal.

A view of Hampton, Virginia, where Washington arrived at age 16 to become a student at Hampton Normal and Agricultural Institute, a model industrial school for blacks. "It seemed to me that it must be the greatest place on earth," he observed, "and not even Heaven presented more attractions for me at that time."

During this period, Booker was sent to work in a nearby coal mine. He hated this job even more than shoveling salt. The work was dirty and exhausting, and according to Booker, there "was always the danger of being blown to pieces by a premature explosion of powder, or of being crushed by falling slate."

One day, while working in the mine, Booker happened to overhear two men talking about a large black school that had recently been established in Virginia. Booker crept up to listen to their conversation. The name of the school was Hampton Normal and Agricultural Institute (*Normal* meaning that it prepared its students to become teachers). Crouching in the darkness, Booker found it hard to imagine a black school any larger or grander than the one in Tinkersville. "I resolved at once to go to [Hampton]," he later wrote, "although I had no idea where it was, or how many miles away, or how I was going to reach it."

Shortly thereafter, Booker heard of a vacant houseboy position in the home of General Lewis Ruffner, one of the wealthiest and most influential men in town. He applied for the job, and to his relief he was hired at five dollars a month. For a while, Booker continued to live with his family, though he eventually moved into the well-appointed Ruffner home.

From the beginning, Booker knew that his job was not going to be easy. The general's wife, Viola Ruffner, had a sharp tongue and a reputation for strictness; few servants were able to live up to her high standards. Booker was determined to keep his position, and he listened carefully as Viola Ruffner explained to him what she expected from her house-boy: "I [learned] that, first of all, she wanted every-thing kept clean about her, that she wanted things done promptly and systematically, and that at the bottom of everything she wanted absolute honesty and frankness. Nothing must be sloven or slipshod; every door, every fence, must be kept in repair."

Booker worked hard to please Viola Ruffner, and they eventually became close friends. Realizing that Booker was a serious and trustworthy young man, Ruffner took it upon herself to further mold his character. She taught him to take pride not only in his work but in his personal appearance. Self-improvement, cleanliness, and good order charac-terized the Ruffner household; during his stay there, Booker was encouraged to adopt these characteristics for himself. As an adult, looking back on his relation-ship with Viola Ruffner, he maintained that the lessons she had taught him as a boy "were as valuable to me as any education I have ever gotten anywhere since."

Viola Ruffner had once been a teacher, and quite naturally she took an interest in Booker's educational pursuit. She provided him with books, and during the winter she allowed him to attend the Tinkersville school for a few hours each day. "He was always willing to quit play for study," she remembered. "He never needed correction or the word 'Hurry!' or 'Come!' for he was always ready for his book." Ruffner also noticed that her houseboy "seemed peculiarly determined to emerge from his obscurity. He was ever restless, uneasy. . . . 'Am I getting on?'—that was his principal question."

In March 1870, the Fifteenth Amendment to the U.S. Constitution was ratified, guaranteeing black men the right to vote. A large parade was held in Charleston to celebrate, and it is likely that Booker was among the thousand blacks who flocked to the city for the daylong festivities.

In 1872, when he was 16, Booker decided to leave the Ruffner household to become a student at Hampton Institute in Virginia. His mother had mixed feelings about his decision. Jane was pleased that her son was ambitious, but at the same time she did not think it was necessary for him to pursue his education. In any event, the family did not have enough money to cover Booker's traveling expenses, let alone his tuition.

Fortunately, help came from an unexpected source. When the black community in Malden heard about Booker's desire to attend Hampton Institute, a collection was taken up. Families gave what they could—a nickel here, a dime there—and before long, enough money had been raised for Booker to begin his journey.

His last hours in Malden were melancholy. Ever since the end of the war, Jane's health had been steadily failing, and as Booker boarded the train for the first leg of his trip, he did not expect to see his mother alive again. "She, however, was very brave through it all," he remembered. (Jane Ferguson died two years later, in the summer of 1874. Booker's brother broke the news to him. It was, Booker recalled, "the saddest and blankest moment in my life.")

Halfway to Hampton, Booker began to run out of money. To his dismay, he had to continue his journey by foot. One evening, he arrived in Richmond, Virginia, tired and hungry. He was still 82 miles from Hampton and flat broke. For several hours, he wandered the streets, peering into store windows, unable to buy even a loaf of bread to satisfy his hunger. Then, by chance, he happened to notice a portion of the board sidewalk that was elevated a foot or two above the street. "I waited for a few minutes," he recalled, "till I was sure that no passers-by could see me, and then crept under the sidewalk and lay for the night upon the ground, with my satchel of clothing for a pillow. Nearly all night I could hear the tramp of feet over my head."

When Booker awoke the next morning, he knew that he had to earn some money to buy food. He happened to be near the wharf, where a large shipment of pig iron was being unloaded. The captain took a liking to him, and for the next week or so, Booker worked as a stevedore until he had saved enough money to continue his journey.

At last, on the morning of October 5, with only a few cents in his pocket, Booker arrived at Hampton Institute. Staring up at the handsome brick building, he was filled with a tremendous sense of pride and accomplishment. "The sight of it seemed to give me new life," he recalled. "I felt that a new kind of existence had now begun—that life would now have a new meaning. I felt that I had reached the promised land." ◖◗

4

HAMPTON INSTITUTE
AND THE DIGNITY
OF LABOR

A photograph of Washington around the time he was enrolled as a student at Hampton Institute. He was so eager to attend the institution that he traveled nearly 200 miles on foot to get there, then paid his way through school by working as a janitor.

LATER THAT DAY—October 5, 1872—Booker T. Washington presented himself before Mary F. Mackie, "lady principal" at Hampton Institute. Washington recalled that Mackie was taken aback by his dirty clothing and his lean, hungry appearance: "I felt that I could hardly blame her if she got the idea that I was a worthless loafer or tramp."

As she did with all new pupils, Mackie asked Washington a few questions about his education. Though she seemed pleased with his answers, she could not decide whether to admit the teenager as a student or not. Washington lingered in her anteroom for more than an hour, nervously waiting for her decision. At last, Mackie turned to him and said briskly, "The adjoining recitation-room needs sweeping. Take the broom and sweep it."

Washington understood at once that this was to be his "entrance exam." Seizing the broom, he swept the recitation room three times. Then, with a thoroughness that Viola Ruffner would have admired, he took a dusting cloth and went over every square inch of woodwork four times. No spot was overlooked.

A bit later, Mackie strode into the room, took out a linen handkerchief, and wiped it across a section of woodwork, then across one of the tables, then along the row of wooden benches. Finally, bending down,

Mary Mackie, the "lady principal" at Hampton Institute, "proved one of my strongest and most helpful friends," according to Washington. Her dedication to black education impressed him to such an extent that he "had no patience with any school for my race in the South which did not teach its students the dignity of labour."

she dragged the delicate hankie across the floor. When it came up clean, Mackie rested her eyes upon Washington. "I guess you will do to enter this institution," she said quietly. "I was one of the happiest souls on earth," Washington remembered.

After Mackie had assigned the new student a room, she discussed with him the matter of finances. Washington was greatly surprised when she told him that his tuition would be paid by an outside source. (He later learned that this was a common practice at Hampton Institute.) Mackie stressed, however, that the students had to cover their own meals, books, and room. These costs, she explained, could be paid in one of two ways: either "wholly by work, or partly by work and partly in cash."

Because Washington had only 50 cents in his pocket, Mackie told him that, if he liked, he could perform janitorial chores to cover his room and board. It sounded like a fair arrangement, and in this way, 16-year-old Washington became Hampton's janitor. "I had a large number of rooms to care for," he later wrote, "and had to work late into the night, while at the same time I had to rise by four o'clock in the morning, in order to build the fires and have a little time in which to prepare my lessons." The work, he admitted, "was hard and taxing, but I stuck to it."

Booker T. Washington stayed at Hampton Institute for three years. Nearly all of the instructors were white, and Washington was continually amazed at the unselfish manner in which these men and women had dedicated their life to the cause of black education. By the end of his first year at Hampton, he had come to the conclusion that "those [individuals] who are happiest are those who do the most for others. This lesson I have tried to carry with me ever since."

Shortly after his arrival at Hampton, Washington met the head of the school, General Samuel Chapman Armstrong. He was instantly struck by the former general's athletic, commanding presence. In Washington's words, Armstrong was "the most perfect specimen of man, physically, mentally and spiritually" he had ever seen. To Washington, the general was "more than a father"; he was, without question, "the noblest, rarest human being that it has ever been my privilege to meet."

Armstrong was 33 years old when Washington first came to Hampton. Intelligent and ambitious, he had been one of the youngest generals to fight in the Civil War. He had founded Hampton Institute in 1869, and to some degree he ran his school like a military academy, complete with morning and evening bells, cadet drills, marching exercises, and daily clothing inspections. "Shoes had to be polished," Washington remembered, "there must be no buttons off the clothing, and no grease-spots."

Armstrong also insisted that his students pay close attention to their hygiene. The general believed that a clean body and a clean mind went hand in hand. Accordingly, Washington became acquainted with the bathtub, the comb, the napkin, and the toothbrush during his first weeks at Hampton.

By nature, Armstrong was cheerful, unselfish, and immensely popular with the female instructors. From the beginning, he took a fatherly interest in the young men and women at Hampton Institute, all of whom were exceptionally fond of him. According to Washington, the general was "worshipped by his students. . . . There is almost no request that he could have made that would not have been complied with."

Despite the close rapport he enjoyed with his students, Armstrong did not believe that blacks and whites were necessarily equals. Most blacks, he felt, were incapable of grasping complex issues and therefore unfit to take an active role in American society.

General Samuel Chapman Armstrong, who founded Hampton Institute and developed its program to instill discipline and morality in students, proved to be the most influential person in Washington's life. "I never met any man," Washington said, "who, in my estimation, was the equal of General Armstrong."

The average black person, he contended, was still "in the early stages of civilization" and inclined to laziness if unsupervised. For this reason, Armstrong and his staff saw to it that the students were kept as busy as possible. "Every hour was occupied in study or work," Washington recalled.

One day was very much like any other at Hampton Institute. Every morning, the students rose at five o'clock for a military drill. Breakfast was served at six. The balance of the day was spent studying a wide variety of subjects: natural philosophy, arithmetic, grammar, geography, history, civil government, moral science, elocution, and bookkeeping. Prayers were held twice a day; there was little time for rest and relaxation. The evening hours, according to Armstrong's wishes, were to be spent "in an atmosphere of Christian influence and sympathy." It was this influence, presumably, that led Washington to become interested in the Bible. He found its lessons deeply inspirational, and for the rest of his life he tried to begin every day by reading a page or two of Scripture.

The majority of Armstrong's students were studying to become schoolteachers. The higher branches of education, however, were not emphasized at Hampton Institute. For the most part, students learned the basics, but not much more. As Armstrong saw it, the strengthening of "character is the true objective point in education." By and large, he believed that blacks lacked not only self-discipline but a sense of morality. And morality, in the general's opinion, was like cement—it held the soul together. Without a sense of morality, a person could never become truly "civilized." This was the primary reason that higher education was not stressed at Hampton Institute—not because the general disapproved of it but because other, more basic things had to be learned first.

At the heart of Hampton's curriculum was what the general called the "routine of industrious habits."

Every student, male and female, was taught that labor was dignified and that great satisfaction (as well as moral improvement) could be derived from performing a task well. Under Armstrong's guidance, Washington wrote, "[I] learned to love labour, not alone for its financial value, but for labour's own sake."

The general also required his students to learn a profession other than teaching. Printing, sewing, carpentry, and shoemaking were a few of the vocations offered. During his three-year stay at the school, Washington learned every aspect of janitorial work.

By teaching his students a practical trade, Armstrong believed he was equipping them with the skills that would allow them to become useful members of society. This, in turn, would gradually earn them the respect and love of their white neighbors. Such was the general's long-range plan for improving race relations in the South. Armstrong also advised his students to rely upon themselves, and not the courts, if they wished to end racial discrimination. "Patience," he wrote, "is better than politics, and industry a shorter road to civil rights, than Congress has in its power to make."

By the end of his third year at Hampton, Washington had eagerly absorbed all of the general's doctrines concerning self-reliance, the dignity of labor, and the importance of personal cleanliness. In addition to these principles, he had acquired a basic elementary school education, had picked up a bit of legal knowledge, and had also learned the art of public speaking, for which he had a natural talent. All in all, Washington considered his education at Hampton equal or superior to any he could have received at Yale or Harvard.

In June 1875, Washington was pleased to be among the graduating students chosen to speak at the Hampton commencement exercises. Before a large and receptive audience, he outlined the various reasons why the island of Cuba, located less than 100

Receiving a well-rounded education through what General Samuel Armstrong described as the "routine of industrious habits," students at Hampton Institute practice their trade skills (opposite page, top), study farming in the classroom (opposite page, bottom), and assemble in military-like formation during a band rehearsal (above). "At that institution," Washington said of his three-year tenure at Hampton, "I got my first taste of what it meant to live a life of unselfishness, my first knowledge of the fact that the happiest individuals are those who do the most to make others useful and happy."

"As a young man," Washington noted in Up from Slavery, *"I used to try to picture in my imagination the feelings and ambitions of a white boy with absolutely no limit placed upon his aspirations and activities. . . . I have [since] learned that success is to be measured not so much by the position that one has reached in life as by the obstacles which he has overcome while trying to succeed."*

miles south of Florida, should not be annexed by the United States. A reporter from the *New York Times* happened to be present, and a day later, the 19-year-old graduate was praised in the *Times* for his "terse, logical and lawyer-like argument" against Cuban annexation.

As the graduating students prepared to leave the institute, Armstrong reminded them to be thrifty and industrious, to vote wisely, to command the respect of their neighbors, and to educate their children. "Remember that you have seen marvellous changes. . . . In view of that be patient—thank God and take courage."

Upon leaving Hampton, Washington returned to his home in Malden. A few months later, he received his teaching certificate, and to his relief he was given a job at the black school in Tinkersville. The salary was low, but Washington was not discouraged. On the contrary, this was, he said later, "the beginning of one of the happiest periods of my life."

At the Tinkersville school, Washington put into practice many of the lessons he had learned under the general. He taught his pupils not only how to read and write but how to polish their boots and comb their hair. Every morning, just as the general had done, Washington inspected his students to make sure that their pants were clean, their jackets buttoned, and their teeth properly brushed. (In time, he became fanatical about the value of the toothbrush—it was, in his words, nothing less than a cornerstone "of civilization.")

In one respect, Washington's educational approach differed slightly from the general's. The head of Hampton Institute was convinced that "the true objective" of any school should be the formation and strengthening of character. Washington's primary goal, however, was to assimilate blacks peacefully into white society—to make the black man "so skilled in

Washington (front row, second from left), General Samuel Armstrong (third row, second from left), Mary Mackie (second row, far left), and other members of Hampton Institute's graduating class of 1875 prepare to have their picture taken on the school grounds. Washington received his diploma (opposite page) from the institute in June 1875, then taught at Tinkersville for three years and studied at a seminary in Washington, D.C., before returning to Hampton in 1879 to serve on its faculty.

of his students would never escape from the coal mines and salt furnaces of the Kanawha Valley. Yet this knowledge, however discouraging, did not prevent him from devoting three years of his life to the communities of Tinkersville and Malden. He worked unselfishly and without complaint. Whenever he felt overworked or unappreciated, he reminded himself that he was toiling not for personal gain but for the betterment of his race—"to help the people of my home town to a higher life," as he phrased it.

In addition to his teaching duties, Washington occasionally involved himself in local politics. During the summer of 1877, for instance, he embarked on a speaking tour, trying to convince the black residents of West Virginia that in the upcoming election Charleston should be chosen as the permanent state capital. A newspaper reporter heard one of Washington's speeches and commended him for expressing "his idea in a clear manner and with appropriate words." On August 7, Charleston was voted the permanent state capital. It was a small victory, politically unimportant, but gradually Washington was learning that he could influence others through the power of his words.

The speaking tour was such a success that for a brief period Washington was tempted to give up his teaching post to pursue a career as a lawyer. In his spare time, he began to study the law, but he eventually abandoned the idea. A law career, he sensed, would be too limiting and not a good use of the broad education he had acquired at Hampton.

Still, Washington was nagged by a feeling of restlessness and indecision. In the summer of 1878, after three years of teaching, he abruptly left his post in Tinkersville and traveled to Washington, D.C., where he enrolled as a student at the Wayland Seminary, a Baptist theological school. His reasons for doing so remain obscure. Washington had never shown much interest in organized religion, and it is unlikely (though not impossible) that he would have decided to give up teaching to become a Baptist minister.

In any event, Washington did not find what he was seeking at the Wayland Seminary. Though he

In 1878, the U.S. government sent 66 Kiowa and Cheyenne Indians to Hampton Institute as part of a project to teach them the ways of American society. Upon joining the Hampton faculty, Washington lived side by side with these Native Americans for more than a year, helping them learn how to adapt to a new culture.

got along well with several of the teachers, he found the curriculum too intellectual and abstract for his taste. The students, he complained, were very handy at Greek and Latin, but they were learning nothing "about life and its conditions."

Washington also felt that many of the students were superficial, more concerned with their clothing and appearance than the quality of their education. It upset him to see young black men who earned no more than four dollars a week hiring buggies on Sunday afternoon "to ride up and down Pennsylvania Avenue in order . . . to convince the world that they were worth thousands." After half a year of religious study, Washington left the seminary in disgust.

Shortly thereafter, in February 1879, Washington received a letter from General Armstrong asking him to return to Hampton to speak at the commencement ceremony in May. Washington agreed, and the rousing speech that he delivered to the graduating class, "The Force That Wins," went over extremely well with students and faculty alike. It was, Washington admitted, "the best address that I was capable of."

A month or so later, he received a second letter from the general asking him to return to Hampton once again, this time to serve on the faculty. "I will allow you $25.00 per month," Armstrong wrote, "for your services here as teacher and assistant in study hour." Washington wrote back at once, accepting the position.

When he began teaching at the institute in the fall of 1879, the school had just entered its 10th year of existence. In educational circles, Hampton was considered a model industrial school, and Washington was proud to be counted among its faculty. And yet, even here, in this safe and familiar environment, there were subtle signs of racial discrimination. Washington's salary was less than that of the white teachers, and he was expected to eat in a separate dining room, away from the other instructors.

Shortly after Washington's arrival, Armstrong asked him to take over the night school, which Washington agreed to do. A small number of students at Hampton were so poor that they had to work all day long to pay their room and board and could only attend school during the evening hours. Naturally, these students were exhausted by the time they got to class, and Washington assumed they would have trouble staying awake while he explained the complexities of civil government.

Happily, this was not the case. Though few in number, the evening students were a bright and highly motivated group. Their eagerness to learn was contagious, and to Washington's surprise, his happiest and most vigorous hours at Hampton were spent in the company of his night students. The atmosphere was so stimulating that Washington's pupils frequently begged him to continue teaching after the "retiring bell" had packed everyone else off to bed.

Appropriately, the night students were nicknamed the Plucky Class, and within a matter of months, evening attendance had more than tripled. In later years, Washington took great pride in the fact that the night school, "which started with only twelve students, now numbers between three and four hundred, and is one of the permanent and most important features of the institution." ❧

5

TUSKEGEE

❦

IN MAY 1881, General Samuel Armstrong received a letter from a group of educational commissioners in Tuskegee, Alabama. Would the general, they asked, be able to recommend a suitable white man to become the principal at their new, tuition-free black school? Armstrong wrote back, saying that at the moment he had no white man to recommend, but if a black man was acceptable, he would send Booker T. Washington, "a very competent capable mulatto. . . . The best man we ever had here."

A week later, during chapel service, the commissioners' reply arrived at Hampton Institute. Armstrong read the telegram aloud before the assembled students: "Booker T. Washington will suit us. Send him at once." "There was," Washington

When Washington arrived in Tuskegee, Alabama, in June 1881 to open a school for blacks, he "expected to find there a building," he said, "and all the necessary apparatus ready for me to begin teaching. To my disappointment, I found nothing of the kind. . . . My first task was to find a place in which to open the school." He chose this site to serve as the home of his school, which he named Tuskegee Institute.

remembered, "a great deal of joy expressed among the students and teachers, and I received very hearty congratulations. I began to get ready at once."

The 25-year-old Washington arrived in the small town of Tuskegee on June 24. He had never visited the Deep South before, and his first impression of Tuskegee, situated at the extreme southern end of the Appalachian mountain chain, was agreeable. The following day, he sent a cheery postcard to his friends at Hampton: "The place has a healthy and pleasant location—high and hilly. Think I shall like it." The seat of Macon County, Tuskegee was a quiet, sleepy town of 2,000 residents, half of whom were black. According to Washington, race relations there were generally pleasant.

Before the Civil War, when cotton had reigned as king, Macon County had been one of the richest regions in the state. But the ravages of the war and the subsequent infiltration of northern money and northern values had changed everything. Throughout the railroad-hungry South, cotton plantations were giving way to steel factories, and Tuskegee had been slipping into economic stagnation for more than a decade.

In February 1881—four months before Washington's arrival—the Alabama state legislature had passed a bill to set aside $2,000 annually to "establish a Normal School for colored teachers at Tuskegee." The businessmen of Macon County hoped that the construction of a black school would stimulate the local economy. They were also hoping that it would stem the flow of local blacks who were leaving Tuskegee in alarming numbers for the wider plains of nearby Kansas.

When Washington arrived at Tuskegee on June 24, he discovered to his surprise that the school had not yet been built. Though the educational bill had been passed in early February, state funding would not be made available until the first of October. To complicate matters, Washington soon learned that the state allocation "could be used only for the payment" of the instructors' salaries and that no provision had been made by the state for the securing of "land, buildings, or apparatus." This meant that for the time being he was unable to purchase books, maps, quills, ink, blackboards, desks, or writing charts—the tools he regarded as essential for providing a proper education. "The task before me," he later wrote, "did not seem a very encouraging one."

But Washington would not admit defeat. Originally, he had planned to open his school in early July, and he was determined to keep to that plan. On June 28, four days after his arrival, he sent a letter to Hampton Institute, requesting whatever books and supplies the school could spare. "You know what I need," he wrote to Hampton's business manager, "and *any thing* that you can send me I will be thankful for."

In the meantime, Washington began to search for a suitable location for his school. Within a few days, he had discovered a 100-acre farm south of town that seemed promising. The land was extremely hilly, and only one-quarter of it had been cleared. On the positive side, there was a large orchard where vegetables could be grown and cotton could be planted. There were also several dilapidated structures that could be turned into small classrooms.

The owner, William Bowen, was willing to sell the farm for $500—$200 to be paid immediately, the balance to be paid within a year's time. Washington wanted to close the deal at once, but, maddeningly, the state allocation could not be used to purchase land. Somehow, he would have to raise the money himself.

In general, the residents of Macon County looked forward to the opening of the new black school. Washington recalled, however, that there were "not

"I confess that what I saw during my month of travel and investigation left me with a very heavy heart," Washington said of his mid-1881 tour through the Alabama countryside to announce the opening of Tuskegee Institute. *"The work to be done in order to lift these people up seemed almost beyond accomplishing."*

Helping construct their own school, students at Tuskegee Institute dig the foundation for the Collis P. Huntington Memorial Building. The edifice was named after the railroad tycoon who donated $2 to the school the first time he met Washington and years later gave 25,000 times that amount. "When Mr. Huntington gave me the first two dollars," Washington remembered, "I did not blame him for not giving me more, but made up my mind that I was going to convince him by tangible results that we were worthy of larger gifts."

a few white people in the vicinity . . . who looked with some disfavour upon the project. They questioned its value to the coloured people, and had a fear that it might result in bringing about trouble between the races."

To alleviate potential hostility, Washington did everything he could to cultivate the goodwill of the Tuskegeans. During his first week in town, he became acquainted with as many people as possible—farmers, businessmen, ministers, schoolteachers, bankers, and physicians. Everywhere he went, he greeted the locals with a handshake and a smile. In his every word and gesture, Washington attempted to make himself appear so useful and so beneficial "that every man, woman and child, white and black, would respect me and want me to live among them."

Shortly after his arrival, Washington learned that there were two black churches in town, one Methodist, the other Baptist. On Sunday, June 26, he appeared before each congregation, explaining to the churchgoers who he was and what he was trying to achieve. The black people of Tuskegee warmly supported the idea of a black school in their community. After the service, they came forward, offering their help and encouragement.

Each afternoon, when Washington returned to his boardinghouse, he found a large number of blacks waiting for him, asking to be enrolled in his school. After giving the matter some thought, he decided that it would be wisest "to receive only those who were above fifteen years of age, and who had previously received some education." The majority of applicants, he discovered, were already public school teachers, many of whom had performed poorly on their state examination. They were hoping that by attending Washington's school they could learn enough to receive a higher grade of teaching certificate, which would allow them to earn more money.

In the end, approximately 30 students were selected for enrollment, half men and half women.

To the astonishment of nearly everyone, Booker T. Washington opened his normal school on July 4, 1881, 10 days after his arrival in Tuskegee. Until the Bowen farm could be purchased, classes were held in a large shack next to the African Methodist Episcopal church. The shanty, as Washington called the shack, was in such poor condition that "whenever it rained, one of the older students would very kindly leave his lessons and hold an umbrella over me while I heard the recitations of the others."

Obviously, this arrangement was inadequate for Washington's purposes. By mid-July, he had managed to borrow $200, enough to make the down payment on the Bowen property. On July 16, he sent a jubilant note to the treasurer of Hampton Institute: "We now have the farm under control." An astute businessman, Washington specified that the land be deeded to the trustees of the school—"not to be held as state property." That way, if the government ever withdrew its funding, the school would not have to close.

Originally, Tuskegee Institute was to have been tuition-free. The paucity of state funding, however, forced Washington to charge his students a small tuition as well as a monthly fee of $8 for their room, meals, and laundry. Keeping in mind the tremendous amount of work that needed to be done on the farm, he set up a labor system identical to the one at Hampton, enabling the students to pay off the cost of their room and board by performing various chores. Most of the pupils at Tuskegee—however grudgingly—took advantage of this arrangement.

As soon as Washington received the deed to the Bowen farm, he and his students began to repair the half-dozen wooden structures, all of which were in pitiful condition. Within a matter of days, the stable and the henhouse were thoroughly cleaned, and with the addition of a few boards and a coat of paint, they were turned into classrooms. A handful of students were put to work building desks, tables, and chairs; others were given the responsibility of nailing down the uneven plank flooring.

In the meantime, the citizens of Tuskegee began dropping by, donating whatever items they thought might be useful. In this way, the school acquired a small supply of blankets, farming implements, and kitchen utensils. To Washington's relief, a shipment of books and newspapers arrived from Hampton Institute.

To make the school as financially independent as possible, Washington decided to plant cotton, which he hoped would provide a steady source of income. Before any planting could be done, however, a large area of land had to be cleared. One day, after class, Washington told everyone to pick up an ax and follow him to the woods. The students stared at him in silence. When they realized that Washington was serious, they made it clear to him that they had come to Tuskegee to become better teachers, not better farmers. In any event, they considered a "cutting bee" undignified.

Washington held his temper. Quietly but firmly, he told his students that manual labor was beneath the dignity of no one. All work, he insisted, was good for the spirit (and, he might have added, good for the school). Then, without another word, he picked up an ax and went outside. A few minutes later, distant chopping could be heard. At that moment, Washington gained the respect of every student at Tuskegee. One by one, they each picked up an ax and headed for the woods to join him.

For the next several weeks, Washington and his pupils worked every afternoon, chopping wood and burning undergrowth, until 20 acres had been cleared. Unfortunately, the land proved to be too hilly and the soil too sandy to produce high-quality cotton. Wisely, the students decided to concentrate their efforts on planting vegetables instead. Before long, a large and healthy garden was thriving on campus.

From the beginning, Washington ran his school very much like Hampton Institute. The Puritan work ethic was strongly emphasized, as was the importance of personal cleanliness. The female students were expected to keep their hair combed and their clothing tidy; the young men had to wear collars and neckties. Everyone became acquainted with the toothbrush.

By November 1881, enrollment at the school had jumped from 30 to 88. The administrative work load became too much for Washington to handle; at his request, instructors from Hampton came to Tuskegee to relieve him of some of the duties. Among the new arrivals was a graceful 27-year-old woman named Olivia Davidson. A talented and clever instructor, she was quickly assigned the post of lady principal.

It was Davidson's uncanny ability to raise money, though, that impressed Washington most. During her first year at Tuskegee, Davidson organized a number of benefits, suppers, and "literary entertainments." She also encouraged her students to go from door to door, soliciting contributions. According to Washington, Davidson "never seemed happy unless she was giving all of her strength to the cause" of black education. Slowly, but surely, the Tuskegee coffers began to fill.

Naturally, the black residents of Macon County took a lively interest in Washington's school. Most of them were too poor to give money, but they contributed what they could: a pig, a quilt, a pitcher of fresh cream. One day, an elderly black woman arrived at the school, dressed in rags. According to Washington, she hobbled forward on a cane and said to him, "I knows what you an' Miss Davidson is tryin'

On August 2, 1882, Washington married Fanny Smith, a former Hampton Institute student who had also been one of his pupils at the Tinkersville school. Their marriage lasted less than two years, however; she died in 1884, a year after giving birth to a daughter, Portia.

Olivia Davidson, the first lady principal at Tuskegee Institute, married Washington in 1885. His second wife, she bore two children: Booker T., Jr., and Ernest. She died in 1889.

to do. . . . I ain't got no money, but I wants you to take dese six eggs, what I's been savin' up, an' I wants you to put dese six eggs into de eddication of dese boys an' gals." Washington was deeply touched by the woman's gift.

Before the school was even a year old, contributions began to arrive in the mail, a large percentage of them from the North. A woman from Boston, for instance, who had donated $35,000 to Hampton Institute, sent $100 to Tuskegee. Washington was careful to keep the school's expenses to a minimum, and by April 1882 the Bowen farm had been completely paid for.

The campus, however, still looked crude and temporary, more like a farm than a school. The converted stable and henhouse could accommodate only a limited number of students, and for the first year, nearly all of Tuskegee's classes were held at the black public school and in the broken-down shanty next to the church.

Boarding was an even greater problem. All of the students at Tuskegee had to live with charitable black families in town, an arrangement that did not suit Washington. Like General Armstrong, he wanted his students to spend all their time at the school, where it would be easier to discipline their behavior and to impress upon them the Puritan virtues of cleanliness and self-help.

As soon as the Bowen farm had been paid for, Washington began to draw up plans for a large wooden building to be erected on campus. As he envisioned it, the building would contain administrative offices and classrooms as well as a dormitory on the third floor for the women students. (For the time being, the young men would continue to live in town.) The cost of construction would run close to $6,000—"a tremendous sum," Washington admitted, but a necessary expenditure. A central building would not only give the school a stronger sense of identity; it would allow Washington and the rest of the faculty to carry out their duties in a more professional manner.

To raise the required money, Washington and Olivia Davidson spent two months touring the northern states, soliciting contributions. Armed with letters of introduction, they called upon the homes of known philanthropists to whom they explained the importance of industrial education. They also spoke before a number of church groups and social organizations. By the end of May 1882, they had collected more than $3,000, enough to begin construction on the new building.

That summer, after the cornerstone had been laid, Washington returned briefly to his hometown of Malden, where he married his longtime sweetheart, Fanny Smith. Years earlier, in 1876, Fanny had been one of his pupils at the Tinkersville school. A bright student, she had later enrolled at Hampton Institute, graduating in May 1882. Three months later, on August 2, she and Washington were married at the Zion Baptist Church in Tinkersville. When Washington returned to his post at Tuskegee, Fanny accompanied him.

Little is known of their married life. According to Washington, his first wife "earnestly devoted her thoughts and time to the work of the school, and was completely one with me in every interest and ambition." Despite her education, Fanny was not assigned any teaching duties at Tuskegee. (The school records list her simply as "Housekeeper.") In 1883, she gave birth to a daughter, Portia. The following year, in the spring of 1884, Fanny Washington died. The cause of her death has eluded biographers, though she may have suffered fatal injuries after falling from a wagon.

At the age of just 28, much to his grief, Booker T. Washington was a widower. ❧

6

BRICK BY BRICK

❧

THE EARLY YEARS of the Tuskegee Normal School were among the busiest and most satisfying of Booker T. Washington's career. The campus continued to enlarge, the faculty and the student body increased, and Washington gradually began to incorporate into the curriculum the fundamentals of industrial education. These were also the years when Washington first began to establish himself not only as a fine educator but as a wise and conservative spokesman for the black race.

In the fall of 1882, after six months of hammering and sawing, the first permanent building was inaugurated at Tuskegee Institute. It was named Porter Hall, after one of the school's most generous donors, businessman Alfred Haynes Porter. In addition to administrative offices, classrooms, and sleeping quarters, the barnlike building contained a library, chapel, dining room, kitchen, laundry, and a small commissary where the students could buy various items. Rising to a height of three stories, Porter Hall was the tallest building in Macon County, and according

After making their own bricks, Tuskegee students stack them for future use. "From the very beginning, at Tuskegee," Washington said, "I was determined to have the students do not only the agricultural and domestic work, but to have them erect their own buildings. My plan was to have them, while performing this service, taught the latest and best methods of labour, so that the school would not only get the benefit of their efforts, but the students themselves would be taught to see not only utility in labour, but beauty and dignity."

Alfred Haynes Porter was one of Tuskegee Institute's most generous donors during the school's early years. Washington used part of the money contributed by the New York businessman to construct what was then the tallest building in Macon County: Porter Hall.

to Washington, "the whites seem about as proud of it as the colored."

The support and encouragement of white Tuskegeans, Washington knew, was vital to the long-term survival of the institute. Week after week, he tried to convince the leery white residents of Macon County that his school was not a threat to the existing social order but rather a vital and beneficial part of the community. As the institute began to receive statewide attention, white Tuskegeans naturally felt a hometown pride, and to Washington's relief, he was regarded as an ally, someone who could be trusted.

If there was one difficulty that characterized the early years of Tuskegee Institute, it was the school's chronic lack of money. As the student body continued to grow, the need for additional buildings and teachers became acute. For increasingly long periods of time, Washington found himself touring the northern cities, trying to raise the necessary funds. He was generally successful, but it was an exhausting and worrisome task.

Fortunately, the school's academic reputation helped lighten the financial burdens. In 1883, only two years after Tuskegee's founding, the Alabama state legislature saw fit to allocate an additional $1,000 a year to cover the instructors' salaries. Almost immediately thereafter, the school received funding from two philanthropic organizations, the Slater Fund for Negro Education and the Peabody Fund, both of which were committed to the cause of black education.

As soon as the school was on firmer ground financially, Washington began to alter the look of the campus and shift the educational emphasis. For the first two years of its existence, the primary function of the institute was to prepare its students to teach in black elementary schools. The courses taught at Tuskegee were for the most part traditional.

In addition to history, geography, and mathematics, the students were encouraged to study literature, astronomy, botany, electricity, bookkeeping, composition, grammar, and penmanship.

Around 1883, however, Washington began to broaden the curriculum, gradually incorporating the fundamentals of industrial education. The changing nature of the school was emphasized in the 1883–84 Tuskegee catalog: "There are hundreds of institutions, North and South, to which students can go and receive extended mental training, but those where young men and women can learn a trade in addition to other training, are few. At present the industries of the institution are farming, brickmaking, carpentering, printing, blacksmithing; and housekeeping and sewing for girls." Within a few years, numerous other vocations were added to the list: cabinetry, shoemaking, painting, broom making, wheelwrighting, mattress making, wagon building, and tinsmithing.

Like his mentor, Samuel Armstrong, Washington saw to it that all the trades offered at his school were relevant to the postwar southern economy. Industrial education, he declared, should "fit us for the work *around* us and demanded by the times in which we live."

· Whenever possible, the academic courses at Tuskegee were given a practical slant. The mathematics students, for instance, were required to measure the length and width of their classroom to determine how much carpet would be needed to cover the floor. In composition class, students were told to write essays on cabinetry, dressmaking, and wheelwrighting. "An ounce of application," Washington once said, "is worth a ton of abstraction."

In keeping with this belief, Latin and Greek were not taught at the institute. Although Washington recognized their academic value, he considered them useless subjects as far as everyday life was concerned. There would be many more occasions, he insisted, when a southern black would need to know how to shoe a horse than to quote the works of Virgil or Ovid.

As mentioned in the school catalog, brickmaking was among the skills offered to the male students at Tuskegee. This trade was not casually introduced into the curriculum; rather, it was a conscious effort on Washington's part to combine his ideas about self-reliance and industrial education. Washington repeatedly told his students that if a black man could offer a useful skill to his community, he would eventually be shown the respect and recognition he deserved "as a man and as a citizen." When deposits of brick clay were discovered on the Tuskegee campus, an opportunity arose for Washington to put this belief into action.

His plan was relatively simple. Washington knew that if the students could make their own bricks, any future buildings on campus could be constructed out of brick, and not wood, thereby ensuring the school's longevity. There was no brickyard in town, and Washington was correct in assuming that any leftover bricks could be sold to the farmers and merchants of Tuskegee, providing a much-needed source of income for the school. Brickmaking would teach the students a trade and would offer visible proof to the local whites that black education was not only beneficial

This wooden structure, which served as Tuskegee Institute's first chapel, was eventually replaced by a brick church. Altogether, 40 buildings were constructed during the school's first 20 years, almost all of them by student labor.

to blacks but to the entire population of Macon County.

Writing to Armstrong, Washington estimated that he and his students could build a kiln and begin to fire bricks for about $200. He was wrong. The first attempt was a disaster: 25,000 handmade bricks refused to burn properly and had to be discarded. The second attempt also failed, for reasons that Washington did not understand. The third experiment was going well until the kiln collapsed in the middle of the night, ruining thousands of bricks.

At this point, the students became quarrelsome; no one could agree on what should be done. The work, Washington remembered, "was hard and dirty, and it was difficult to get the students to help. . . . More than one man became disgusted and left the school."

Washington refused to give up, however. In his mind, brickmaking became symbolic of everything he was trying to achieve at the institute. To raise additional money, he pawned his watch for $15, and ignoring the protests of others, he and a handful of students set about reconstructing the collapsed kiln. To everyone's relief, the fourth attempt at brickmaking was successful. From then on, all of the buildings on campus were constructed of handmade brick, and the people of Tuskegee began to order bricks in great quantities from the institute. (By 1900, the kiln was turning out more than a million high-quality bricks a year, which were sold for a good price throughout Macon County.)

During this period of growth and progress, Washington brought his brother, John, and John's wife, Susie, to Tuskegee. After graduating from Hampton, John had worked briefly as a teacher at the black school in Tinkersville. He had later found employment with the U.S. Corps of Engineers, which had assigned him a succession of low-paying, menial jobs.

John welcomed the move to Tuskegee, where he acted as business agent for a salary of $30 a month.

In 1885, one year after the death of his wife, Washington married the institute's lady principal, Olivia Davidson. Her commitment to the school was as strong as Washington's, and it is not difficult to understand their mutual attraction. Despite Olivia's often frail condition, she bore two children: Booker T. Washington, Jr., nicknamed "Baker" (born in 1885), and Ernest Davidson Washington (born in 1889).

"During our married life," Washington wrote, "[Olivia] continued to divide her time and strength between our home and the work for the school. She . . . also kept up her habit of going North to secure funds." As lady principal, Olivia took an active interest in the female students at Tuskegee. In a motherly way, she reminded them to keep up their appearance and maintain an air of decency in their actions. When a group of young women went into town, she warned them not to loiter in saloons, dip snuff, gossip, or listen to off-color jokes.

In addition to her work at the institute, Olivia traveled around Macon County, meeting with groups of rural women and trying, with some success, to organize reading societies and home-improvement clubs. "She literally wore herself out," Washington remembered, "in her never ceasing efforts in behalf of the work that she so dearly loved."

It was also during this period, around 1885, that Washington began to establish himself as a spokesman for the black race. Just as he had done at his school in Tinkersville, he encouraged his students to assimilate themselves peacefully into southern white society. This, Washington believed, was the safest and most prudent course for blacks to take. While he admitted that "the Negro is a much stronger and wiser man than he was" during slavery, he could still not "afford to act in a manner that will alienate his Southern white neighbours from him."

With this conciliatory attitude, it is easy to understand why many whites supported Washington's beliefs, sought out his company, and contributed money to his school. His racial ideas sounded reasonable and nonthreatening, and before long he was winning friends in high places, especially in the Alabama legislature, which continued to appropriate ever-increasing sums to Tuskegee Institute. As early as 1883, Washington's efforts were being praised on the floor of the U.S. Senate. In time, state officials began to seek out Washington's advice, and during his first years at Tuskegee, he was able to make recommendations that improved the quality of black education in many parts of the South.

In July 1884, Washington was invited to speak at the annual meeting of the National Education Association (NEA) in Madison, Wisconsin. To the surprise of his audience, he did not confine his speech to educational issues but chose instead to tackle "the broad question of the relations of the two races."

The matter, as he saw it, was extremely simple: "Any movement for the elevation of the Southern Negro, in order to be successful, must have to a certain extent the cooperation of the Southern whites." Washington assured his listeners that southern blacks were anxious to contribute to society, that southern whites were good and decent people, and that the answer to racial strife lay in the continuing education of black men and women. "Good school-teachers and plenty of money to pay them," he said, "will be more potent in settling the race question than many civil rights bills and investigating committees."

Though he did not explicitly say so, Washington had little or no faith in federal legislation as far as black progress was concerned. A year earlier, in 1883, the U.S. Supreme Court had struck down as uncon-

Wheelwrighting (opposite page, top), printing (opposite page, bottom), and mattress making (above) were just a few of the trades students learned at Tuskegee Institute. "The individual," Washington said, "who can do something that the world wants done will, in the end, make his way regardless of his race."

stitutional the Civil Rights Act of 1875, which had guaranteed black citizens the right to equal treatment in theaters, inns, and other public facilities. The Supreme Court ruling was a crushing blow to blacks throughout America. "We have been, as a class, grievously wounded," said Frederick Douglass, the nation's most distinguished black spokesman. At the NEA meeting, Washington did not challenge the court's ruling; on the other hand, his emphasis on black self-reliance seemed more timely than ever.

In his speech, delivered before 4,000 black and white educators, Washington showed that he was a pragmatist, not an idealist. As a black man and former slave, he thought he knew exactly where he stood in relation to the southern whites and how best to overcome their feelings of prejudice. Most comforting to whites, he appeared to place the responsibility for black progress squarely on the shoulders of the black people themselves. "Brains, property, and character for the Negro," Washington declared, "will settle the question of civil rights."

It was an effective speech, delivered by a man who was becoming remarkably adept at public relations. Washington later called his appearance at the NEA meeting "the beginning of my public-speaking career."

During the months that followed, Washington received a number of speaking invitations from groups throughout the North. He accepted as many as he could, often combining these engagements with fund-raising trips. Many white northerners, he discovered, were curious to hear his opinions on racial matters, and the more he spoke, the more he had to clarify in his own mind exactly how he felt about the troublesome issue of race relations.

As his schedule became increasingly hectic, Washington did not seem to realize that he was pushing himself too hard. In addition to his speaking engagements, he was teaching at his school, making all of Tuskegee's administrative decisions, overseeing campus construction, trying to raise a family, and, with the help of his wife, touring the northern states to raise funds. He was also devoting some of his time and energy to the Alabama State Teachers Association, which he had helped found in 1882.

The strain proved too much. Shortly after his wedding, in October 1885, Washington suffered a nervous collapse that kept him in bed for 10 days. "He is not as strong, physically, as he was two years ago," Olivia wrote to a friend, "and I am sure it is due to his close application to his work." From Hampton Institute, General Armstrong sent his former pupil a stern warning: "You are in some risk of a break down—if your health fails your position will be bad!"

But it was Olivia's health that failed first. Even before coming to Tuskegee, her condition had been strangely frail. On several occasions, she had checked herself into the hospital, but each time, to her dismay, the doctors were unable to determine the nature of her illness. After the birth of her second son, Ernest, Olivia's frailty became so severe that she was moved to Massachusetts General Hospital in Boston, where she died three months later, on May 9, 1889.

Washington was profoundly grieved by the death of his second wife. During the weeks and months that followed, his friends and colleagues noticed that he had taken on a new sadness, and for the first time in his life his thoughts became cynical. Nothing seemed certain anymore. He and Olivia had planned to spend their life together working side by side, and now she had been taken from him, suddenly and for no apparent purpose. He did not understand, and he would never be the same man again. ✸

7

A PRIVATE MAN

B Y 1890, BOOKER T. Washington had become a popular speaker on the educational circuit. "His style is mostly conversational," observed one northern listener. "Now and then as he becomes especially eloquent his voice rises and his form expands. . . . He has a limitless store of original anecdotes gleaned from personal experience with which he keeps his audience in a constant roar." Laughter (often at the expense of blacks) was an important component of Washington's speeches.

Because he was unpretentious in his public manner, many whites assumed that Booker T. Washington was a simple man. This was not the case. There were many aspects of his personality that were not immediately apparent to his listeners—that, indeed, did not become fully known until decades after his death.

"There is a thread of sympathy and oneness that connects a . . . speaker with his audience," Washington said, "that is just as strong as though it was something tangible and visible. If in an audience of a thousand people there is one person who is not in sympathy with my views, or is inclined to be doubtful, cold, or critical, I can pick him out. When I have found him I usually go straight at him, and it is a great satisfaction to watch the process of his thawing out."

Washington constantly encouraged philanthropists and politicians to visit Tuskegee Institute, well aware that everyone who came to the school was generally impressed by its neatness and order. To make sure things remained that way, he was constantly on the lookout for signs of untidiness when he made his daily rounds through the dining hall (above), the classrooms (opposite page), and the rest of the campus.

Although Washington came across as warm and folksy when speaking to an audience, many of his students found him cold and distant. A stern administrator, he was more likely to point out a student's faults than to praise his or her accomplishments. Washington, moreover, tended to be suspicious of anyone who did not support his plans wholeheartedly. If a student or a member of the faculty disagreed with him, he or she was expected to keep silent, at least in public. In the privacy of his office, Washington would listen to anyone's complaint, but in the end he ran his school exactly as he wished.

Those who knew Washington well may have noticed that his private behavior did not always match his public statements. Though he frequently advised his students to stay away from politics, Washington could not resist the lure of bureaucracy. He enjoyed conversing with state officials, making educational recommendations, and, most of all, quietly pulling strings to ensure a political appointment or to hinder unfavorable legislation. There was yet another side to his personality that would have surprised many people. Despite his fervent support of black education, Washington could be competitive and even unfriendly toward rival black universities.

When he learned in 1887, for instance, that a black state college was thinking of relocating to Montgomery, Alabama—only 40 miles from Tuskegee—Washington felt threatened. He feared that the new school would steal away his student body and possibly affect the $3,000 he was receiving each year from the state legislature. Working quietly and taking only a few people into his confidence, he did everything he could to make sure that the relocation did not happen. He wrote letters, hired a lobbyist to put pressure on the governor of Alabama, and purchased the editorial support of a black newspaper. He also slipped money into the pockets of those politicians he felt could most effectively redirect the school elsewhere.

To Washington's disappointment, Montgomery was chosen as the new site for the state college. "We will waste no time worrying over it," Washington advised one of his teachers, "but throw our energy toward making Tuskegee all the better." Politically, the incident was unimportant; it did, however, reveal much about Washington's personality, his fears, and his early reliance on behind-the-scenes maneuvering. This secrecy would become increasingly important to him in the years ahead.

In the summer of 1890, Washington was invited to speak to the graduating students at Fisk University, a black school in Nashville, Tennessee. For his subject, the 34-year-old educator chose "The Colored Ministry: Its Defects and Needs." In this speech, Washington asserted that the black ministry was hopelessly out of touch with the rural masses and that the majority of black ministers were for the most part uneducated. He also claimed that the average minister was far more concerned with his salary than the salvation of his congregation. In his most blistering statement, Washington asserted that "three-fourths of the Baptist ministers and two-thirds of the Methodists are unfit, either mentally or morally, or both, to preach the Gospel to any one or attempt to lead any one."

Washington's speech, which was published a few weeks later in the black press, created a fire storm of controversy. Theologians, in particular, were outraged by his caustic remarks. To the surprise of many people, Washington refused to retract any of his statements. In a letter to an Indianapolis newspaper, he insisted that he was not attacking organized religion; he was only attempting to separate ministers into two groups, "the upright and the immoral, the

Washington's brother John and his sister-in-law Susie gather for a family portrait outside their Tuskegee home. Following in his younger brother's footsteps, John attended Hampton Institute and taught at the black school in Tinkersville before arriving at Tuskegee, where he acted as business agent for the institute.

weak and the strong." The more he tried to explain himself, however, the angrier his foes must have become.

To this day, historians have been unable to explain satisfactorily why Washington should have chosen this moment to attack the colored ministry. As a black educator eager to secure the favor of whites, one of his guiding principles was to avoid any form of notoriety; now, for a brief moment, he seemed to be inviting it. Perhaps he was still distraught over the death of his wife Olivia; perhaps, for fund-raising purposes, he was trying to prove to northerners that his school was not affiliated with any organized religion.

If so, the result was ironic. Shortly after his speech, two wealthy sisters, Olivia and Caroline Stokes, endowed Tuskegee Institute with a $2,000 scholarship fund. The money, they instructed Washington, was to be used "to help in the education of colored men of good moral character, particularly those who have the ministry in view." Later, the

Stokes sisters contributed enough money to build a small chapel on the Tuskegee campus as well as a Bible school for the training of future ministers.

To Washington's relief, the repercussions from his Nashville speech were short-lived. Within a few months, the controversy had died down, and he was able once again to devote his full attention to his administrative duties at Tuskegee. By this time, the school had developed an excellent reputation academically, and Washington was often held up in educational circles as an outstanding example of black progress.

To generate additional publicity for the institute, Washington constantly encouraged philanthropists and politicians to visit the school whenever they liked. Those who came to Tuskegee were usually impressed by what they saw, and this, in turn, reflected well on Washington. An Alabama legislator went so far as to call him "one of the best men in the United States," a rare compliment for a white man to pay a black man in the 1890s. When the editors of *Outlook* magazine compiled a list of the nation's 28 leading college presidents, Washington's name was prominently featured, along with the presidents of Harvard, Yale, and Princeton universities.

Despite these accolades for Washington and his school, the importance of black education was not generally heeded in the South. The state of Alabama, in particular, was extremely poor, and many of its citizens questioned the wisdom of allocating $3,000 a year to the institute. There were others in Alabama who were vehemently opposed to any form of state-supported black education, and legislation was regularly introduced to abolish all funding for it. These skeptics, therefore, must have been irritated that Washington ran his school in a professional and thrifty manner. No dollar was ever wasted at Tuskegee Institute.

To further mollify his critics, Washington was extremely careful not to antagonize the local whites. The cordial relationship that existed between his students and the whites of Macon County was understandably delicate and could easily be damaged by a thoughtless remark or indiscreet action. To prevent this from happening, Washington closely monitored the behavior of his students. When they had occasion to go into town, he told them to mind their manners, to show respect to the white shopkeepers, and to avoid at all costs any discussion that would "tend to stir up strife between the races."

For many years, this policy served Washington well. If, for some reason, a student attempted to challenge it, the educator was known to react swiftly. In 1887, one of his graduates began publishing a newspaper in the town of Tuskegee that contained, according to the *Montgomery Advertiser*, "incendiary articles against the white race." In no uncertain terms, Washington requested that *The Black Belt* cease publication. Students who persisted in uttering statements of an "agitating character" were advised to leave the school. Such occurrences were rare, however, and most pupils were content to follow Washington's patient and peaceful example.

In 1891, the school celebrated its 10th anniversary. Looking around, Washington could feel proud of what he had accomplished. The size of the campus had increased dramatically, from 100 acres to nearly 540. The number of students had also jumped, from 30 to more than 500. There were many new buildings on campus; the vegetable gardens and barnyards were thriving; the brickyard was turning out thousands of quality bricks daily. As a symbol of black progress, the student-built water tower rose 65 feet into the air, the highest point in Macon County. The students were even publishing their own bulletin, the *Southern Letter*, which enjoyed a wide readership among Tus-

Margaret James Murray came to Tuskegee Institute as an English teacher in 1889, shortly after the death of Washington's second wife, Olivia. Murray was appointed lady principal the following year and married Washington in 1892. Years later, in 1904, the Washingtons adopted Margaret's orphaned niece, Laura Murray.

kegee's growing circle of friends. A casual observer could see that the institute was no longer a tiny rural school; it had, in fact, become a small town.

As the campus continued to grow in size, the financial burdens increased proportionately. To his annoyance, Washington found himself on the road for weeks at a time, calling upon northern businessmen, trying to convince them to contribute money toward the cause of black education. Because he was so frequently away from home, the task of raising his three children fell to his brother, John, and his sister-in-law, Susie. During this period, Washington's adopted brother, James, also came to live at Tuskegee. James brought his wife and children with him, and over the years he served in various positions, including teacher, postmaster, and part-time football coach. A friendly and humorous man, he became a well-liked member of the Tuskegee community.

In the autumn of 1892, Washington married for the third and final time. His wife was 27-year-old Margaret James Murray. Maggie, as she was often called, had come to Tuskegee as an English teacher in 1889, shortly after Olivia's death. A year later, in 1890, she was appointed lady principal. A graduate of Fisk University, Maggie was a witty and well-groomed mulatto woman who shared Washington's conservative views and his commitment to black education. Like most people, she was intimidated at first by the formality of Washington's speech and bearing; even after they had become intimate, she had trouble calling him by his first name.

On the whole, the Washingtons' marriage was a peaceful and happy one. Without much complaint, Maggie cared for her stepchildren, accompanied her husband on his fund-raising trips, and, as head of women's industries, supervised the female students at Tuskegee. In later years, after the children had grown, she became active in numerous black women's organizations, eventually serving as president of the National Federation of Colored Women's Clubs.

While he was busy working to establish Tuskegee Institute as an industrial school for blacks, Washington (standing on podium, in middle ground) emerged as a popular speaker on the educational circuit. "I do not believe," Washington once said, "that one should speak unless, deep down in his heart, he feels convinced that he has a message to deliver."

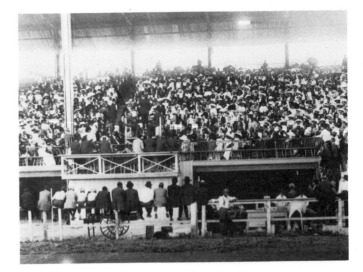

In 1893, General Samuel Armstrong paid a two-month visit to Tuskegee. Washington must have been shocked by his mentor's appearance: Two years earlier, Armstrong had suffered a massive stroke that had paralyzed much of his body. When he spoke, his words were garbled and difficult to understand. He was no longer able to walk and had to be moved about in a wheelchair. Nevertheless, the students at the institute stood in awe of the 54-year-old educator. They had heard Armstrong's praises sung so often that to many he seemed an almost mythic figure.

Despite the general's frailty, his mind was still alert, and as he toured the campus, he was extremely pleased with the progress that Washington had made with his students. The self-help philosophy was alive and well at Tuskegee. "[Washington] is kind, just and fair," Armstrong reported to his own pupils upon returning to Hampton. "If you find something not right in the world, act as Mr. Washington has."

A few months later, Washington received word that the general had died. He was deeply grieved, and for the rest of his life he did everything he could to keep alive the memory of Hampton's distinguished founder. "[Armstrong] was, in my opinion, the rarest, strongest, and most beautiful character that it has ever been my privilege to meet," he later wrote in his autobiography. ". . . One might have removed from Hampton all the buildings, class-rooms, teachers, and industries, and given the men and women there the opportunity of coming into daily contact with General Armstrong, and that alone would have been a liberal education."

8

"A SAFE LEADER"

◄◖◗►

IN THE AUTUMN of 1895, Booker T. Washington was invited to speak at the Cotton States and International Exposition in Atlanta. The speech that he delivered, which came to be known as the Atlanta Compromise, was not particularly original, but it was forceful and timely. Addressing an audience of several thousand people, Washington acknowledged that it would be "folly" for black southerners to agitate for civil rights at the present time. Social equality would eventually be granted to blacks, he said, but any privileges that "come to us must be the result of severe and constant struggle rather than of artificial forcing." The Atlanta audience understood "artificial forcing" to mean laws or constitutional amendments, any legal device that would allow blacks to obtain their civil rights. Murmurs of white approval could be heard throughout the auditorium.

Halfway through his address, Washington tackled the issue of racial animosity in the South. There was a painless solution to the race problem, he implied, one that required no change in the existing social order. "In all things that are purely social," he said, "we can be as separate as the fingers"—here he raised his hand, each finger clearly separated from its neighbor—"yet one as the hand in all things essential

Tuskegee students work in the 10-acre experiment station, part of the agriculture school established at the institute in 1896. Most of the experiments conducted at the station were designed to help southern farmers improve their crop yield. In 1897, the Slater-Armstrong Agricultural Building was inaugurated at Tuskegee.

to mutual progress." Dramatically, his fingers closed together in a fist of solidarity and power.

Washington finished his speech by urging southern whites to give their black neighbors a fair chance to compete in the economic marketplace. By working together, he said, black hand joined with white, a new period of prosperity and racial harmony would be delivered "into our beloved South." According to one person in the audience, "an ovation followed [such] as I had never seen before and never expect to see again." Hats and canes were waved in the air; women hurled flowers onto the stage. The multitude, said one reporter, "was in an uproar of enthusiasm. . . . It was as if the orator had bewitched them."

It was not until the following day, however, that Washington began to realize how deeply his words had affected the citizens of Atlanta. As he walked through the business district, people pointed him out. Soon, he was surrounded by a crowd of men eager to shake his hand. "This was kept up on every street on to which I went," Washington recalled. Embarrassed, he hurried back to his boardinghouse.

The newspapers, meanwhile, were treating his Atlanta address as a major story. "The speech of Booker T. Washington . . . seems to have dwarfed all the other proceedings and the Exposition itself," said the *Boston Transcript*. "The sensation that it has caused in the press has never been equalled." According to one southern editor, Washington's address was "the beginning of a moral revolution in America." The *Atlanta Constitution* perhaps summed it up best: "The speech stamps Booker T. Washington as a wise counselor and a safe leader."

The text of the Atlanta Compromise was widely reprinted in newspapers, and within a short time Washington had come to be regarded by whites and blacks alike as the successor to Frederick Douglass, who had died a few months earlier. It was an honor that took Washington by surprise. "I never had the remotest idea that I should be selected or looked upon . . . as a leader of the Negro people," he later confessed.

Shortly after returning to Tuskegee, Washington received a letter from President Grover Cleveland. "I have read [your speech] with intense interest," the president wrote from his home in Buzzards Bay, Massachusetts. "Your words cannot fail to delight and encourage all who wish well for your race." Cleveland and Washington soon became good friends; according to Washington, the president contributed money to Tuskegee Institute and used his influence to secure the donations of others.

By mid-October, the volume of Washington's mail had increased dramatically. Every week, he received letters and telegrams from newspaper editors asking him to submit articles. He was also besieged with numerous offers from lecture bureaus across the country. "To all these communications," he later wrote, "I replied that my life-work was at Tuskegee; and that whenever I spoke it must be in the interests of the Tuskegee school and my race, and that I would enter into no arrangements that seemed to place a mere commercial value upon my services."

Most of Washington's speeches for the next 20 years were simply variations on his Atlanta Compromise address. Again and again, he reminded southern blacks to become educated and to stop "fretting and fussing" over the issue of civil rights. He was telling white Americans exactly what they wanted to hear, and for this reason he was regarded as an unusually wise man. Wherever he spoke, the auditorium was filled to capacity.

Black Americans, on the other hand, were not sure how they felt about the Great Accommodator, as Washington was being called. Naturally, some blacks were thrilled by his success. "It looks as if you are our Douglass," declared T. Thomas Fortune, editor of the *New York Age*, "the best equipped of the

Frederick Douglass remained America's most powerful black spokesman for half a century. His death on February 20, 1895, cleared the way for a new leader of the black race to emerge. Washington seized the opportunity seven months later, when he delivered his landmark address, the Atlanta Compromise.

lot of us to be the single figure ahead of the procession."

Other blacks were decidedly less enthused. They felt that Washington had been too accommodating in Atlanta, too willing to sacrifice black dignity for the short-term benefits of economic opportunity and interracial harmony. "He said something that was death to the Afro-American and elevating to the white people," railed the editor of the *Washington Bee.* Another newspaper, the *Atlanta Advocate,* minced no words: "We doubt if the Tuskegee normal school will receive any benefit from Prof. Bad Taste's sycophantic attitude but there is no doubt in our minds that his race will suffer."

Usually, Washington was able to steer clear of his adversaries—but not always. In May 1896, the governor of Alabama, William Oates, was invited to speak at the Tuskegee commencement. He used the opportunity to dash cold water on any hopes that may have been raised by the Atlanta Compromise. "I want to give you niggers a few words of plain talk and advice," he told the assembled students. "You might as well understand that this is a white man's country, as far as the South is concerned, and we are going to make you keep your place. Understand that. I have nothing more to say to you."

To avert an ugly situation, Washington cut short the rest of the ceremony. "Ladies and gentlemen," he said good-naturedly, "I am sure you will agree with me that we have had enough eloquence for one occasion. . . . We will now rise, sing the doxology, and be dismissed." Washington had no desire to pick a fight with Governor Oates. Confrontation was not his style.

A month later, in June 1896, Harvard University conferred upon Washington an honorary master of arts degree, the first time the eastern school had given this distinction to a black. Receiving the degree, Washington recalled, was "the greatest surprise that

On June 24, 1896, Washington became the first black to receive an honorary master of arts degree from Harvard University. This well-publicized event led to visits to other prominent universities, including Yale (below), which invited him to attend its bicentennial celebration.

ever came to me." The event was well publicized and did much to enhance his reputation as a wise and conservative black leader. A Boston newspaper was careful to note that the Harvard degree had been conferred upon Washington not because he "is a coloured man, or because he was born in slavery, but because he has shown . . . a genius and a broad humanity which count for greatness in any man, whether his skin be white or black."

As Washington's prestige continued to increase, it became easier for him to attract the attention of northern philanthropists, who began to associate the success of the black race with the success of Washington's school. Nearly every department at Tuskegee benefited from northern philanthropy, but it was in the field of agriculture that the results were most rewarding.

For nearly 15 years, Washington had hoped to make the study of agriculture an important part of the Tuskegee program, but to his regret he had never been able to secure the necessary funding. In 1896, the Slater Fund for Negro Education provided the institute with enough money to establish a separate agricultural school. At once, Washington began to look for a suitable black man to run the department, finally settling on a 31-year-old agriculturist named George Washington Carver.

At the moment, Carver was teaching at Iowa State College and working toward his master's degree in agriculture. Naturally, he was flattered to receive Washington's invitation to teach at Tuskegee. He hesitated to accept, however, explaining that he wanted to finish his degree first. Washington agreed to wait, and to sweeten the deal, he offered Carver a yearly salary of $1,000 plus board—considerably more than most teachers at Tuskegee were receiving. In his letter of acceptance, Carver wrote, "I am looking forward to a very busy, very pleasant and profitable time at your college."

Agriculturist George Washington Carver joined the Tuskegee faculty in 1896 and remained on the staff for nearly 50 years. He believed that the type of education offered at Tuskegee was "the key to unlock the golden door of freedom" to southern blacks.

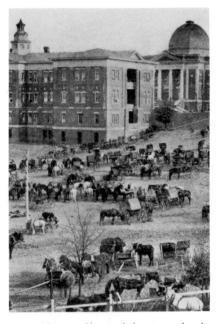

Teams of horses belonging to local farmers attending the Tuskegee Negro Conference line the institute's campus. Washington established the annual conference in 1892 to extend the benefits of Tuskegee's education program to blacks who were not enrolled there.

Upon arriving at Tuskegee in the fall of 1896, Carver was assigned an unusually heavy work load. In addition to overseeing the new agriculture department, he was expected to run the school's two farms; direct a 10-acre agricultural experiment station; and teach classes in botany, chemistry, and agricultural science. It was also understood that Carver would function as Tuskegee's veterinarian and, in his spare time, do what he could to beautify the campus.

Though he had every reason to feel overworked, Carver did not complain. It was well known among the faculty that Washington had no patience for whiners; lazy teachers at Tuskegee soon found themselves looking for a new job. Keeping this in mind, Carver did everything he could to please Washington, and within a year's time he had established himself as one of Tuskegee's most popular and inspirational teachers.

Carver was fascinated by all aspects of agricultural research, and years later his work in that field would bring international recognition to Tuskegee Institute. During his first decade at the school, Carver carried out dozens of scientific experiments, most of them designed to help southern farmers improve their crop yield. In the laboratory and in the fields, he studied different varieties of cotton, tested organic fertilizers, and tried to discover ways to restore worn-out soil. His observations were published in a series of easy-to-read bulletins that received wide distribution in the South. These publications were especially valuable to black farmers, the majority of whom were unaware of the various ways in which they could improve their methods of farming.

To Washington's pleasure, Carver also became a guiding force of the Tuskegee Negro Conference, an annual gathering of farmers that Washington had inaugurated a few years earlier, in 1892. Here, at Tuskegee Institute, black sharecroppers were able to obtain advice on a variety of agricultural issues. Many of the farmers were already familiar with Carver's experiments through his bulletins and were eager to hear what he had to say. Carver showed the men his experiment station, held simple demonstrations, and did his best to answer their questions concerning fertilization and crop diversity. He even passed out free seeds, which had been supplied to the school by the U.S. Department of Agriculture.

In time, the Tuskegee Negro Conference became an important forum for blacks throughout the South. Washington usually served as chairman, and throughout the day he acted as the voice of black self-help. He urged the farmers to buy land; to raise more food supplies; to keep out of debt; and to send their children to school, if only for a few months each year. A tiny amount of education, Washington insisted, was better than none.

At each gathering, Washington tried to learn as much as he could about the farmers. He asked them detailed questions about their families, their schools, their churches, their burial services. He wanted to know whether or not they could read, how large their cabins were, and how many black people in their district were allowed to vote. In this way, he was able to reacquaint himself on a yearly basis with the true condition of southern black life—information he needed to know if he was to effectively serve as spokesman for the black race.

Naturally, Washington used the Tuskegee Negro Conferences to promote his ideas concerning black accommodation. By and large, the farmers, ministers, and schoolteachers who attended the annual event were receptive to his message. According to one participant, Washington's racial philosophy sounded extremely reasonable: "Keep out of politics, make any concession consistent with manhood. Let white men know you are glad you are a Negro. Don't push, but be proud of your blood." ❧

9

DINNER AT THE WHITE HOUSE

❦

IN THE AUTUMN of 1898, Booker T. Washington was invited to make a speech at the Chicago Peace Jubilee, a large event celebrating the end of the Spanish-American War. On the evening of October 16, Washington spoke to a capacity crowd of 16,000 people. Among the dignitaries present, he recalled, were President William McKinley, "the members of his Cabinet, many foreign ministers, and a large number of army and navy officers, many of whom had distinguished themselves in the war which had just closed."

On this occasion, Washington's words were more forceful than usual. Taking advantage of the patriotic mood, he spoke of the numerous times when black soldiers had fought valiantly in defense of the United States. A race that was willing to die for its country, Washington declared, should also "be given the highest opportunity to live for its country." Racial prejudice, he went on to say, was "a cancer gnawing at the heart of the Republic, that shall one day prove

In the early 1900s, Washington emerged as an important adviser to President Theodore Roosevelt (standing), especially in the matter of appointing blacks to political office. The alliance benefited both men: The educator helped Roosevelt choose for office blacks who could strengthen his political party; the president, in turn, assisted Washington in establishing a network of loyal supporters who could help him achieve his political goals.

Washington arrives in Copenhagen, Denmark, as a guest of the Danish royal family during his three-month tour of Europe in 1899. The trip marked his first extended vacation since he founded Tuskegee Institute 18 years earlier.

as dangerous as an attack from an army without or within."

During his stay in Chicago, Washington lunched twice with McKinley's presidential party, a breach of social custom that annoyed many people. Several newspaper editors put Washington on the spot, demanding to know whether he believed blacks and whites should mingle socially. Washington's answer was guarded. Both races, he responded, "have enough problems pressing upon us for solution without adding a social question, out of which nothing but harm would come." He added that prejudice was "something to be lived down not talked down." The incident quickly passed from public memory, though it foreshadowed a much more controversial event that would occur three years later, during Theodore Roosevelt's administration.

In the spring of 1899, Washington traveled to Europe with his wife Maggie. By this time, his hectic schedule was beginning to take its toll. Physically, Washington felt drained, and he welcomed the prospect of an extended vacation. As the steamship pulled away from the harbor, he remembered, the load of "responsibility which I had carried for eighteen years began to lift itself from my shoulders at the rate, it seemed to me, of a pound a minute." Washington's exhaustion was so extreme that he slept for 15 hours a day for the next 30 days.

While in Europe, he and his wife met with a variety of celebrities and world leaders, including writer Mark Twain, painter Henry Tanner, feminist Susan B. Anthony, and African explorer Sir Henry M. Stanley. In Paris, Washington was the guest of honor at a banquet attended by former president Benjamin Harrison. In London, he paid a visit to Windsor Castle, where he had tea with Queen Victoria. During his stay in England, he also addressed numerous schools and social organizations, including the Women's Liberal Club and the Royal College for the Blind.

Washington thoroughly enjoyed his three-month European holiday, an experience that broadened his outlook and strengthened his already formidable public reputation. Yet he could not entirely forget his worries at home. A few days before he departed for Europe, a brutal lynching had taken place in Palmetto, Georgia. A black man, Sam Hose, had been accused of rape and murder, and the infuriated white residents of Palmetto had strung him from a tree and burned him alive. The charred pieces of the body were later distributed among the populace.

Blacks throughout the nation were horrified by the incident, and before leaving for Europe, Washington was asked to make a public statement. Aware of the delicacy of his position, he refused to do so. "I feel constrained to keep silent," he told reporters, "and not engage in any controversy that might react on the work to which I am now lending my efforts." He did add, however, that education would offer "the permanent cure" for such ugly behavior as lynching.

This was not the answer that most blacks wanted to hear. A few months later, Washington's ambivalent response to the Hose murder was hotly debated at the annual meeting of the Afro-American Council, a militant black organization founded in 1898. (The Council, in turn, was an offshoot of an earlier group known as the Afro-American League, of which Washington had been a nonparticipating member.) Upon returning from Europe, in August 1899, Washington traveled to Chicago, where the annual meeting was taking place. His friends, however, recommended that he stay away from the convention, which he did.

Within the committee room of the Afro-American Council, there was angry talk of passing a resolution against Washington for not attending the meeting. A white reporter happened to be present at one of the evening sessions, and soon it was being reported in white newspapers across the nation that the Afro-American Council had formally repudiated Washington and his racial philosophy.

This report alarmed the leading members of the council, who hastened to assure the white press that the story was inaccurate, that the council firmly supported Washington's good work on behalf of the black race. Washington, meanwhile, had traveled to Saratoga to deliver a speech. There he put an end to the controversy by assuring reporters that when he had left Chicago, there had been "the very happiest understanding" between himself and the members of the council.

Privately, however, Washington knew that his standing with the Afro-American Council had been seriously jeopardized. He decided, therefore, to create his own organization, the National Negro Business League (NNBL), which held its first annual meeting in August 1900. The purpose of the NNBL was to promote the achievements of black businessmen, to protect consumers against fraud, and to teach enterprising but poor blacks how to gain an economic foothold in society.

Washington (front row, center) at the first annual meeting of the National Negro Business League, which was held on August 22, 1900, in Boston, Massachusetts. By 1905, 300 branches of the organization had been established in the United States.

Though Washington would not admit it, his idea for the NNBL had been borrowed from a similar division of the Afro-American Council. That league had died a quick death, the victim of infighting and misunderstandings. Washington's group, on the other hand, was an immediate success. More than 300 professionals attended the first meeting in Boston, and within a few years, NNBL branches were being founded in major cities across the country. For black entrepreneurs, the league proved to be an effective method of obtaining practical information and advice; for Washington, it would serve as a useful instrument to guard himself against his critics, most of whom were congregated in the North.

In a further effort to solidify his role as a black spokesman, Washington wrote several books during this period, including two autobiographies. The first, *The Story of My Life and Work* (1900), was ruined by hasty writing and sloppy copyediting. His second autobiography, however, has come to be recognized as an American classic.

In *Up from Slavery* (1901), Washington recounted the story of his life, from his birth near Hale's Ford, Virginia, to his European visit in 1899. For social historians, the book has the added value of presenting, in a clear and forceful style, Washington's ideas

Industrialist Andrew Carnegie (above) and feminist Susan B. Anthony (opposite page) were among the most prominent speakers to appear at Tuskegee Institute. Because the school was a showcase of industrial education, it attracted a steady stream of visitors.

concerning the black man's place in American life—ideas that were occasionally diluted or altered by turn-of-the-century newspaper reporters.

Unlike his first autobiography, *Up from Slavery* is a compelling rags-to-riches story, told with warmth and wisdom and numerous anecdotes. Many critics called it one of the most important books of the year. It was "stimulating," "stirring," "one of the most cheerful, hopeful books that we have had the privilege to read."

If *Up from Slavery* holds any fault for today's reader, it is Washington's presentation of himself. On nearly every page, he is extraordinarily patient, always willing to forgive and forget, never harboring a grudge or allowing his emotions to get the better of him. These are not necessarily bad qualities, but there is a saintliness to his character that can sometimes be wearying.

Financially, *Up from Slavery* was a modest success. Its sales were never astonishing, but it continued to be popular for many years, long after other best-sellers had gone out of print. People from all walks of life were deeply moved by the Tuskegee educator's struggle and eventual triumph. "I want to tell you what an immediate influence [your book] had on our nine year old boy," one woman wrote to Washington. "He showed me with great pride, the other day, a rack . . . he'd been making of hard wood, and said 'I'd never have got that more than half done, mother, if I hadn't kept thinking all the time how Booker Washington made up his mind he'd do things!'"

During Washington's lifetime, *Up from Slavery* was translated into many languages, including Swedish, German, Zulu, Russian, Chinese, Arabic, and Braille. The book was especially popular in India, where it was used as a text in some schools. To this day, *Up from Slavery* can be found in numerous paperback editions; among historians, it is regarded as one of the most inspiring books ever written by a black American.

The success of Washington's autobiography brought a certain measure of financial stability to Tuskegee Institute. The book found its way into the hands of numerous philanthropists, many of whom had never given much thought to the cause of black education. The response of George Eastman, a wealthy camera manufacturer, was typical. "I have just been re-reading your book," he wrote to Washington, ". . . and have come to the conclusion that I cannot dispose of five thousand dollars to any better advantage than to send it to you for your Institute." (Years later, after Washington's death, Eastman contributed $250,000 to Tuskegee's memorial fund.)

By the autumn of 1901, Washington had reached the apex of his distinguished career. He was respected by whites and blacks alike, and his educational work at Tuskegee was often praised in newspapers and magazine articles. Nearly 1,100 pupils were enrolled at the school, and the total worth of Tuskegee's assets exceeded $325,000. Because of his fame and his enviable budget, Washington was able to bring to his school some of the nation's finest black instructors. He was also able to attract a number of notable speakers, including Secretary of War William Howard Taft and industrialist Andrew Carnegie.

One of the most popular speakers to appear at Tuskegee was feminist Susan B. Anthony, who paid a visit to the campus in the spring of 1903. According to the school paper, "The welcome accorded Miss Anthony was warm and enthusiastic to the last degree, a sea of snowy handkerchiefs greeting her with the 'Chautauqua salute' when she arose to begin her address." The 83-year-old feminist had followed the school's progress for many years, and before leaving, she promised to raise $100 for the new broom factory that Washington was hoping to build.

Despite the calm atmosphere depicted in this illustration, Washington's October 16, 1901, dinner with President Theodore Roosevelt at the White House created a storm of controversy. The dinner caused both men to be attacked in the white press—especially Washington, who had promised that the races could remain as separate as the fingers "in all things that are purely social."

Perhaps the greatest honor of Washington's life occurred in October 1901, when he was invited to dine with President Theodore Roosevelt at the White House. A popular and charismatic leader, Roosevelt had known Washington for several years, and on more than one occasion he had solicited Washington's advice on matters of racial importance. Roosevelt confessed to a friend that he had felt a moment's hesitation about inviting a black man to dine at the White House; then, feeling ashamed of himself, he sent the invitation.

Washington arrived in the nation's capital on the afternoon of October 16, and that evening he dined with the president and the first family. After supper, Washington and Roosevelt discussed a variety of issues, including black and white relations in the South. The conversation went well, and a few hours later, Washington departed by train for New York City.

Two days later, when the story was printed in the press, there was an immediate public outcry. Most whites, especially those in the South, were shocked at the idea of a black dining at the White House with the president. Even white liberals drew back in amazement—it seemed incredible to them that Roosevelt was consulting a black man on matters of national importance.

Black leaders, of course, were very pleased. They saw the White House dinner as a significant step forward in the fight against racism, and the president's action was warmly praised by the black press. Roosevelt, meanwhile, was surprised that the dinner was creating such a stir. Sending an invitation to Washington, he recalled, had seemed to him "so natural and so proper."

While it lasted, the debate over the White House dinner was intense. For weeks, Washington was pestered by reporters, all of whom demanded a statement. When he refused to answer any questions, the *Brooklyn Eagle* printed a fake interview, putting words into Washington's mouth. The *Richmond Times* went so far as to suggest that, by inviting a black man to the White House, Roosevelt was subtly advocating interracial marriage—an appalling idea to most white Americans.

Roosevelt did what he could to defend himself. Privately, he saw nothing wrong with the dinner, and it saddened him that the White House should be off limits to a distinguished citizen simply because of skin color. After giving the matter considerable thought, the president was unable to decide if he had made a mistake by inviting Washington to dinner. "Looking back," he confided to a friend, "it may be that it was not worth while to consult him. Yet I am not sure."

One thing, however, was clear: Never again did Roosevelt invite Washington, or any other black person, to the White House.

10

WASHINGTON AND HIS CRITICS

Washington stands behind several members of the Tuskegee Machine, the influential group of politicians, businessmen, philanthropists, and educators who helped advance the Tuskegee president's views on black affairs by spreading his doctrines, promoting those who thought as he did, and sabotaging the careers of his opponents. "After a time," said another black leader, W.E.B. Du Bois, "almost no Negro institution could collect funds without the recommendation or acquiescence of Mr. Washington."

Despite the controversy that Booker T. Washington's dining at the White House had caused, it solidified his position as the most important black man in America, the undisputed leader of his race. Even his critics were temporarily stilled. Bishop Henry M. Turner, who had earlier lashed out against Washington's moderate racial policy, was now full of enthusiastic admiration. "You are about to be the great representative and hero of the Negro race," he wrote to Washington. ". . .I thank you, thank you, thank you."

For the next several years, Washington quietly continued to advise President Theodore Roosevelt, especially in the matter of appointing blacks to minor government positions. The educator was pleased when Roosevelt agreed with him that a black man, William Crum, should be made collector of the port at Charleston, South Carolina. Crum's appointment, however, set off a bitter debate among members of the Senate, who wanted to give the post to a white man. Roosevelt refused to give in to his opponents, and after a two-year battle, he managed to persuade Congress to confirm Crum's appointment. Washington was elated.

97

South Carolina senator Ben Tillman was part of an influential group of southern Republicans, known as the Lily-Whites, who sought to eliminate blacks from almost every arena of American politics. Washington constantly found himself locked in battle with these white supremacists as he lobbied to get blacks appointed to political office in the early 1900s.

In many respects, however, his alliance with Roosevelt was frustrating. The president acted upon some of Washington's suggestions, but he ignored others, and there were occasions when the educator feared that Roosevelt was not acting in the best interests of the black race. During one conversation, their words became so heated that Washington feared "that there might be a break between [Roosevelt] and myself."

Although the president liked and respected Washington, he did not wish to associate himself too closely with the controversial issue of black civil rights. An experienced politician, Roosevelt knew that if he wanted to be reelected to office in 1904, he would need the support of the Lily-Whites, an influential group of southern Republicans who, during the 1890s, had successfully eliminated blacks from almost every arena of American politics. They had managed to do this through a discriminatory, yet legal, process known as disfranchisement.

Ratified in 1870, the Fifteenth Amendment prohibited states from denying the vote on the basis of race. After its passage, a large number of black men in the United States began to vote, enjoying for the first time a measure of political equality. Beginning in 1890, however, southern white politicians passed a series of legal measures that made it almost impossible for blacks to vote. By 1910, the South had effectively disfranchised almost all its black residents.

Washington had mixed feelings about the subject. He believed that the property-holding class of blacks should be allowed to vote but that the majority of poor blacks (and poor whites, for that matter) were too uneducated to be responsible voters. Nevertheless, he did what he could to stem the tide of disfranchisement, working behind the scenes and banding together those politicians who might make a difference.

In 1899, Washington and his supporters attacked a disfranchisement bill facing the Georgia legislature. To their disgust, they received almost no support from the black population they were trying to help. "I have been corresponding with leading people in the state but cannot stir up a single colored man to take the lead in trying to head off this movement," Washington complained to his friend T. Thomas Fortune. ". . .They will not even answer my letters."

Washington continued the fight, however, and to his astonishment, the Georgia bill was defeated, 137 to 3. According to Fortune, it was "the only substantial victory we have had in the South in a long time."

Two years later, in 1901, the issue of disfranchisement was debated at the Alabama Constitutional Convention. This time, Washington's strategy was less successful. A few days before the convention opened, he met with a small group of conservative blacks and drew up a statement that was meant to calm the fears of bigoted whites in Alabama: "The Negro is not seeking to rule the white man. The Negro does ask, however, that since he is taxed . . . , is punished for crime, [and] is called upon to defend his country, that he have some humble share in choosing those who shall rule over him, especially when he has proven his worthiness by becoming a tax-payer and a worthy, reliable citizen."

The statement failed to achieve its purpose: Disfranchisement was legally adopted in Alabama. Recognizing defeat, Washington chose to remain silent. As he later explained to British novelist H. G. Wells, "The only answer to it all is for coloured men to be patient, to make themselves competent, to do good work, [and] to live well." (Then again, Washington could afford to be patient. He was one of the few black men in Macon County who continued to vote despite disfranchisement.)

By 1903, a growing number of blacks were beginning to criticize Washington's plodding approach to the race problem. The social harmony he had promised in Atlanta had not come to pass. Lynchings had not been eradicated; railway cars and other public places were still segregated; and each year, disfranchisement inched its way farther north. Gradually, black politicians were becoming a thing of the past. There were no black senators, no black governors; in some states, blacks were not even allowed to attend conventions as delegates. For all practical purposes, black Americans had lost their political voice. They looked to Booker T. Washington to protect their interests and came away disappointed.

In July 1903, Washington was scheduled to speak at a black church in Boston. It was a hot night, and the feisty crowd, peppered with Washington's opponents, was in no mood to hear his speech. "We don't like you," someone shouted from the back. A moment later, catcalls and hissing began. Several fistfights broke out and one man was stabbed before police were able to break up the melee. Dozens of newspapers seized upon the story, and for the first time, whites became aware of the serious breach that was beginning to form within the ranks of America's black leadership.

Privately, Washington was deeply disturbed by the Boston riot. Publicly, however, he shrugged it off as a matter of no importance: "The mere fact that I know there is a group here and there watching for mistakes on my part makes me more valuable I think to the race."

As opposition to Washington continued to mount, the black community gradually splintered into two factions. One camp, the Bookerites, believed that Washington was doing everything he could for the race; the other camp, consisting largely of northern, college-educated blacks, maintained that the

Great Accommodator was an embarrassment and a hindrance to black progress. William Monroe Trotter, outspoken cofounder of the *Boston Guardian*, fell into the latter camp. "Is the rope and the torch all the race is to get under [Washington's] leadership?" he demanded. In September 1903, there was even talk among Trotter's associates of assassinating Washington in a Cambridge, Massachusetts, church where he was scheduled to speak. The plot was discovered, however, and the conspirators fled in fear.

After the Boston riot, Washington began to adopt a variety of tactics to protect himself against his opponents. He made every effort to suppress articles in black newspapers that were critical of his leadership. He also started up three newspapers of his own, all of which were designed to showcase Tuskegee Institute and his own racial philosophy. Espionage formed an important part of Washington's strategy. He wanted to know what his critics were doing, when and where they were meeting, and what was being said about him behind his back.

By 1904, Washington had surrounded himself with a large group of loyal supporters who could be depended upon to supply him with the information he needed. This network, which came to be known as the Tuskegee Machine, had tentacles extending as far as Chicago and as high as the White House. For Washington, the Machine served as an effective system for rewarding his friends and sabotaging the careers of his enemies. Among his "lieutenants," Washington was regarded with a mixture of respect and fear. One of his spies, Melvin Chisum, was in the habit of addressing him as "your Eminence." More commonly, Washington was referred to as "the Wizard" (though never to his face).

Paranoia lubricated the gears of the Tuskegee Machine. Washington went so far as to draw up a list of his enemies, men who were attempting to thwart

William Monroe Trotter was cofounder and editor of the Boston Guardian, *a black weekly newspaper that savagely attacked Washington's accommodationist policies. Tensions between the two men reached a head on July 30, 1903, when Trotter led a disturbance at a black church where Washington was scheduled to speak.*

Originally an admirer of Washington's, W. E. B. Du Bois emerged as his chief rival in 1903 after publishing "a frank evaluation" of the Tuskegee president in The Souls of Black Folk. In the book's opening chapter, "Of Mr. Booker T. Washington and Others," Du Bois criticized Washington's industrial program as "a gospel of work and money" that denied "the higher aims of life" and "tended to shift the burden of the Negro problem to the Negro's shoulders."

his racial policy and topple him from his lofty position of power. One of the names on his list was William Edward Burghardt Du Bois, a member of the faculty at Atlanta University. Washington was convinced that Du Bois had been one of the ringleaders behind the riot in Boston (although this does not appear to have been the case).

A decade earlier, Du Bois had warmly supported Washington's address at the Atlanta Exposition, claiming that it "might be the basis of a real settlement between whites and blacks in the South." Around 1902, however, Du Bois began to agree with Washington's critics, among them William Monroe Trotter, who had been arrested and jailed for his participation in the Boston riot. Du Bois did not necessarily agree with Trotter's tactics, but he could not help admiring the Boston journalist's "indomitable energy."

In 1903, Du Bois's third book was published, *The Souls of Black Folk*, an incisive collection of essays examining various aspects of black culture. The chapter that caught everyone's attention was entitled "Of Mr. Booker T. Washington and Others." In this essay, Du Bois attempted to analyze Washington's platform and why it was an ineffective solution to the race problem. While admiring some of Washington's self-help ideas, Du Bois criticized his "unnecessarily narrow" vision as far as black education was concerned. By discouraging blacks from attending college, Du Bois asserted, Washington was stunting the intellectual growth of the race. He also disapproved of Washington's mild-mannered response to such injustices as lynching and segregation. "We have no right to sit silently by," Du Bois wrote, "while the inevitable seeds are sown for a harvest of disaster to our children, black and white."

The Souls of Black Folk was warmly reviewed by the national press, and within the black community people began to speak of the Trotter–Du Bois faction (though after the Boston riot and his subsequent jail sentence, Trotter's credibility was temporarily destroyed). Du Bois's followers tended to be young northern intellectuals, black men and women who were eager to overthrow Washington's "namby-pamby policy" of accommodation. Picking up where Trotter had left off, Du Bois declared that the time had come for blacks to demand their civil rights in a straightforward and unequivocal way. To act otherwise, he said, would do a great disservice not only to blacks but to the nation as a whole.

Naturally, Washington distrusted Du Bois and his faction, whom he regarded as "a noisy, turbulent and unscrupulous set of men." Washington was a pragmatist, however; he knew he would have to act quickly to avoid a bitter power struggle, one that might result in public humiliation. In January 1904, he invited his supporters and his opponents to come together for a three-day meeting at Carnegie Hall in New York City. The conference, according to Washington, would offer the two sides a chance "to agree upon certain fundamental principles and to see in what way we . . . misunderstand each other and correct mistakes as far as possible."

Du Bois took a dim view of the event and at first refused to come. "The conference is yours," he wrote to Washington, "and you will naturally constitute it as you choose." The 36-year-old scholar and activist had no desire to participate in what he called a "BTW ratification meeting."

Although Du Bois eventually changed his mind, the Carnegie Hall conference was not a success. Neither side trusted the other, and when the meeting came to a close on January 8, nothing substantial had been achieved—the two camps were as far apart as ever. Washington, however, deluded himself by refusing to acknowledge that a serious breach continued to exist. "I am quite sure," he wrote to a friend, "that several of the members, perhaps the majority of those

Seeking to bridge the gap among the nation's black leaders, Washington arranged a three-day conference in January 1904 between his supporters and opponents at New York City's Carnegie Hall. According to W. E. B. Du Bois and other Washington critics, the conference proved to be little more than a "BTW ratification meeting," with the Tuskegee president and his followers seizing control of the proceedings.

who have been in opposition, are either silenced or won over to see the error of their way. There were others of whom this cannot be said, but will have to be watched in the future." He was referring, of course, to Du Bois, who for the next decade would continue to be Washington's harshest and most eloquent critic.

There were few racial issues upon which the two men could agree. On the subject of black voting rights, the Tuskegee educator acknowledged the injustice of disfranchisement, but he also recognized that for the time being there was nothing he could do about it. Du Bois, on the other hand, was outraged by the actions of the Lily-Whites. He maintained that "in a democratic republic the right to vote is of paramount importance" and that until all black men were able to cast ballots, he and his supporters would "never cease to protest and assail the ears of America."

On educational matters, Washington and Du Bois were not as far apart as they seemed to think. Du Bois basically supported the idea of industrial education, but as both a Fisk and Harvard graduate, his sympathies naturally lay with those students who sought advanced education. He called them the "Talented Tenth," the 10 percent of college-educated black Americans who "must be made leaders of thought and missionaries of culture among their people." Washington, however, was more concerned with the nine-tenths of black Americans who needed to learn to read and write and master some industry that would allow them to become "worthy, reliable" citizens.

Unfortunately for Washington, his attitude toward higher education was largely misunderstood. In his speeches and writings, he tried to make it clear that he was not opposed to black men and women going to college. (Indeed, his daughter, Portia, had enrolled at Wellesley College in the fall of 1901.) Still, Washington did not believe it was necessary for the majority of blacks to do so.

Personal experience, moreover, had convinced him that most university graduates were a spineless lot. This, he felt, was particularly true of Du Bois and his followers. "In most cases," Washington wrote to Theodore Roosevelt, "someone has taken these men up and coddled them by paying their way through college. At Tuskegee a man works for everything that he gets, hence we turn out real men instead of artificial ones."

With such fundamental differences in outlook, it was inevitable that Du Bois and Washington would regard each other as enemies. In July 1905, 18 months after the failure of the Carnegie Hall conference, Du Bois and his compatriots founded a civil rights organization known as the Niagara Movement. As Du Bois envisioned it, the all-black movement would provide "aggressive action on the part of men who believe in Negro freedom and growth." The first meeting, attended by 29 black intellectuals, took place at Fort Erie, Ontario, near Niagara Falls.

After much discussion, Du Bois, Trotter, and their colleagues drew up a straightforward declaration of principles, which was printed a few days later in the *Boston Transcript*. The most far-reaching of Niagara's objectives was "the abolition of all caste distinctions based simply on race or color." Du Bois's group was

Eighteen months after the failure of the January 1904 conference at Carnegie Hall, W. E. B. Du Bois (seated, left) founded the Niagara Movement to oppose Washington's accommodationist policies through "organized determination and aggressive action." The Tuskegee Machine, however, encountered few problems in containing Du Bois, William Monroe Trotter (seated, right), and the other black activists who attended the Niagara Movement's third annual conference, in Boston.

also committed to "freedom of speech and criticism," a clear warning to Washington and the members of the Tuskegee Machine.

The formation of the Niagara Movement troubled Washington. At first, he tried to ignore it, and he encouraged the press to do the same. "The best of the white newspapers in the North have . . . taken no account of its meetings or its protestations," reported Washington's private secretary, Emmett Scott. It was Scott's belief that by refusing "to take the slightest notice of [the Niagara Movement] that the whole thing will die aborning."

Washington's secretary was wrong. When the Niagara Movement met for its second annual meeting, in the summer of 1906, it boasted a membership of 170—small compared to the Tuskegee Machine but large enough to irritate Washington, who sent one of his lieutenants to spy on the proceedings. The meeting took place at Harpers Ferry, West Virginia, where in 1859 the abolitionist John Brown had tried, unsuccessfully, to lead a slave rebellion. From this symbolic setting, Du Bois and his followers issued a blunt proclamation: "We claim for ourselves every right that belongs to freeborn Americans—political, civil and social. . . . We want full manhood suffrage, and we want it now, henceforth and forever."

The meeting at Harpers Ferry was widely covered by the press, and Washington was forced to admit that it would no longer be practical to ignore Du Bois and his "scoundrels," as he called them. The real purpose of the Niagara Movement, Washington was convinced, was "to defeat and oppose every thing I do." He felt justified, then, in using any tactic to crush Du Bois, Trotter, and the others. He sent spies to infiltrate Niagara's meetings. He attempted to suppress a black magazine that was showing signs of becoming a mouthpiece for Niagara's philosophy. He even hired detectives to investigate the personal life of various Niagara members.

Washington's tactics were successful. Despite its militant tone (or perhaps because of it), the Niagara Movement failed to achieve any importance as a civil rights organization. The few victories that Du Bois enjoyed were for the most part inconsequential. Too much of his time was spent fighting the Bookerites, and this left little opportunity for tackling the bigger issues of segregation and disfranchisement. By confining its membership to the Talented Tenth, the Niagara Movement alienated itself from middle- and lower-class blacks, most of whom continued to subscribe to Washington's self-help philosophy. Nor did the Niagara Movement have a central headquarters, a paid staff, or the financial support of influential whites, as did Washington. In almost every respect, Du Bois's organization was poorly positioned to carry out its noble objectives.

Thirty years later, Du Bois admitted that he was partly to blame for the collapse of the Niagara Movement, which formally disbanded in 1910. "I was no natural leader of men," he wrote in his book *Dusk of Dawn*. "I could not slap people on the back and make friends of strangers." But Booker T. Washington could, and the Tuskegee Machine rolled on, leaving in its wake W. E. B. Du Bois and the wreckage of the Niagara Movement. ❧

11

"THE MODERN MOSES"

BOOKER T. WASHINGTON never enjoyed much of a family life. He spent half his time on the train, traveling from one city to another, checking in and out of boardinghouses, sifting through his correspondence, preparing speeches, giving newspaper interviews, and meeting with black community leaders. He rarely wrote to his wife or children when he was on the road, relying instead on his private secretary, Emmett Scott, to keep him informed of all that was happening at Tuskegee. When he was at home, Washington was too often preoccupied with his work to pay close attention to family matters.

"We joke . . . about father's silence," his daughter, Portia, told the *Boston Globe* in 1901. "I suppose he is thinking always of the work when he is at home. But the public sees him at his best. When he loses himself in his subject he is much more animated than in the family circle."

Beginning in 1905, Washington embarked on a series of well-publicized state tours. As one historian

In April 1906, Tuskegee Institute celebrated its 25th anniversary with the help of several distinguished guests. Heading the list of speakers were Harvard University president Charles Eliot (right) and wealthy industrialist Andrew Carnegie (second from right); together, they represented Washington's ties to America's cultural and economic leaders.

Washington with three of his four children (clockwise from top left): Ernest Davidson (nicknamed Dave); Booker T., Jr., (nicknamed Baker); and his adopted daughter, Laura Murray. He also had another daughter, Portia.

has noted, oratory "was the chief form of public entertainment in Washington's day, and he almost always put on a good show." The news that Washington's train was approaching the station was enough to generate plenty of interest and excitement. Most Americans were eager to see the Great Accommodator in person, and the churches, banquet halls, and fraternal lodges were usually packed when he spoke.

Just as he had done in the past, Washington often combined his speaking engagements with fundraising trips. In the northern cities of Philadelphia, Boston, and Chicago, he sought out white philanthropists to whom he explained the value of black education and the good work being done at Tuskegee. Many of these businessmen were already familiar with Washington's accomplishments through *Up from Slavery*; reaching for their pocketbooks, they assured him they were eager to do what they could for the advancement of the black race. The abuses that were regularly heaped upon Washington by his black critics meant little or nothing to his white supporters, the majority of whom had never heard of W. E. B. Du Bois or the Niagara Movement.

During the final 15 years of Washington's life, a number of distinguished millionaires donated money to Tuskegee Institute, most notably John D. Rockefeller and Andrew Carnegie, both of whom lived in New York. Considering his humble origin, Washington felt surprisingly at ease associating with the movers and shakers of American capitalism. There was nothing extraordinary about his ability to raise funds. As Du Bois shrewdly observed, when Washington called upon a philanthropist, "he sat there and found out what the white man wanted him to say, and then as soon as possible he said it."

Oil millionaire John D. Rockefeller never visited Tuskegee, but each year he donated $10,000 toward its support. In 1902, a handsome brick building was erected on campus named Rockefeller Hall. Washington made every effort to keep down the cost of construction, and when the last brick had been laid, he returned $249 to Rockefeller's son, explaining that the building had not gone over budget. John, Jr., was impressed by Washington's honesty, and, politely, he refused to accept the money.

Andrew Carnegie was another multimillionaire who had enjoyed reading *Up from Slavery.* The steel baron admired Washington's self-help philosophy, and beginning in 1902, he gave $10,000 a year to the institute. He also supplied the funds for a two-story brick library, which the Tuskegee students built themselves.

In April 1903, a Tuskegee fund-raising rally was held at Madison Square Garden in New York. Among the guests present were former president Grover Cleveland and Andrew Carnegie. Before this moneyed crowd, Washington chose his words carefully. "You of the North owe an unfulfilled duty to the Negro," he declared, "and equal duty to your white brethren in the South in assisting them to help to remove the load of ignorance resting upon my race." Later that evening, Andrew Carnegie passed forward a slip of paper agreeing to give the school $600,000—a tremendous sum in 1903—but only if Washington was willing to set aside $150,000 for his personal needs.

Washington was deeply moved by Carnegie's generosity, but the $150,000 gift troubled him. He feared—with justification—that it would affect his ability to raise funds in the future and that it might inflame the resentment of his white southern neighbors. After giving the matter considerable thought, he and two of his trustees made an appointment to visit Carnegie at his New York mansion. There Washington explained that he could not possibly accept such a large sum for his own use. Carnegie listened in silence; then, nodding, he said, "You go back there into my library, re-write my pledge to suit yourselves, bring it back to me and I'll sign it." Washington did so, and the deal was concluded.

Carnegie had nothing but admiration for the self-made educator, author, and racial diplomat. "To me," he wrote at the time, "[Washington] seems one of the foremost of living men because his work is unique. The modern Moses, who leads his race and lifts it through Education to even better and higher things. . . . History is to know two Washingtons, one white, the other black, both Fathers of their People."

Carnegie's endowment considerably eased the financial burdens of Tuskegee Institute. The money also allowed Washington to treat himself to a well-deserved European vacation. Before his departure from New York in September 1903, the newspapers reported that his health was failing. The 47-year-old educator vigorously denied it. "As a matter of fact," he told the press, "my general health was never better, but I have had no vacation, and a number of my friends have insisted that I take a short trip to Europe. I have yielded to their wishes, but shall return on the same ship I sail upon, and shall not be gone longer than three weeks altogether." Washington had a way of making even his vacations sound structured and businesslike.

Upon returning to the States in mid-October, Washington continued his work with renewed ener-

Standing between Washington and his wife Margaret, President Theodore Roosevelt attends a ceremony in honor of his visit to Tuskegee Institute. "I question whether any man ever went into the Presidency," Washington said, "with a more sincere desire to be of real service to the South than Mr. Roosevelt did."

gy. Though much of his attention after 1903 was devoted to his ongoing battle with Du Bois, Washington did not allow himself to forget that his primary contribution to the race was his educational work at Tuskegee. Even when he was on the road, he managed to keep a close eye on everything that was happening at the institute. Firing off detailed telegrams to Emmett Scott, Washington wanted to know how well the students were eating; what books the teachers were reading in their spare time; how many eggs the chickens were laying; and how sanitary the kitchens and outhouses were. Scott kept no secrets from the Wizard; if someone at Tuskegee was breaking the rules, Washington was sure to find out.

Around 1905, the administration decided that the industrial aspect of the institute needed to be more strongly emphasized. It was thus announced to the faculty that Tuskegee was going to become "a first class industrial school rather than a second class academic." Naturally, this frustrated the academic teachers, who considered literature more important than wheelwrighting and blacksmithing. Though Washington did not realize it at the time, the shift in curriculum only served to intensify the feelings of jealousy and ill will that already existed between the two departments.

Many instructors, moreover, resented Washington's insistence on what he called "dovetailing," his long-standing belief that industrial and academic studies should be combined whenever possible (composition students writing about brickmaking, for instance). One of the academic teachers, Ruth Anna Fisher, absolutely refused to compromise her work in this way. She was promptly asked by Washington to hand in her resignation.

There were other sources of faculty bitterness as well. Washington set unusually high standards for himself and everyone around him, and he did not hide his disapproval when a teacher failed to live up to his expectations. In an angry letter to his pastor, an instructor, G. David Houston, complained about Washington's oppressive personality: "[His] scheme is to have such a control over his teachers that they will tremble at his approach. Most teachers like to see the train puff out with him and dread to hear the engine whistling his return. Relying upon his absolute power, he reserves the right to discharge a teacher at any time. . . . This is not all, he haunts that teacher forever." (Somehow, a copy of this letter fell into Washington's hands, much to Houston's regret.)

Under these circumstances, it is not surprising that most teachers refrained from criticizing Washington, even in private. Good teaching jobs were hard to come by, and they had no desire to begin looking for another one. Most instructors at Tuskegee held their tongue and did their best to "dovetail."

Fortunately for Washington, the public was unaware of any discord that existed at his school. Every year, hundreds of visitors flocked to the institute, and nearly all came away with the impression that it was a southern oasis of harmony, intelligence, and racial goodwill. Usually, visitors were shown around the campus grounds, then taken through the classrooms and industrial workrooms, where they watched the students repair wagons, iron linen, and grind cane into syrup. In the afternoon, Maggie Washington invited the guests to pause for tea and light refreshments. Later, as the shadows began to lengthen, the visitors were taken to the chapel, where a group of students sang spirituals and other plantation songs. A plentiful dinner was served before the visitors departed. The overall atmosphere of efficiency and cleanliness surprised outsiders, most of whom had expected to find at least some degree of squalor at an all-black institution.

Foreigners were especially fascinated by what they saw at Tuskegee. *Up from Slavery* had been translated

Washington heads the commencement day exercises at Tuskegee Institute. By the time of its 25th anniversary, the school had gained such a lofty reputation that people came from as far away as China to see it.

into most major languages, and a surprising number of Cubans, Puerto Ricans, Haitians, and Jamaicans showed up at the school, asking to be enrolled. Tourists from Japan and China were also in the habit of dropping in, eager to observe Tuskegee's educational and agricultural practices.

In April 1906, the institute celebrated its 25th anniversary. Thousands of southerners came by train, horse, and wagon to join in the festivities. Andrew Carnegie was one of the keynote speakers; to no one's surprise, he talked about wealth. "Money may be the root of all evil," he acknowledged, ". . . but it is also the root of all Universities, Colleges, Churches and libraries scattered thru the land." Carnegie then stressed the importance of education, assuring the students that as soon as they were properly educated, "all rights will . . . be added unto you in this country."

Another speaker that day was Secretary of War William Howard Taft. The 48-year-old Republican's speech was less optimistic than Carnegie's. While praising the industrial work that was being performed at Tuskegee, Taft declared that blacks were "not fit to enjoy or maintain the higher education." There were many blacks in the audience who believed that Taft would become the next president of the United States, and his racist observation must have caused a momentary feeling of dismay to settle over the otherwise jubilant crowd. ❧

12

"LEADING THE WAY BACKWARD"

Washington in his Tuskegee Institute office attends to some paperwork with the help of his private secretary, Emmett Scott. As Washington's right-hand man, Scott oversaw the office staff, spied on its faculty, served as his press secretary and ghostwriter, and represented him at important meetings when the educator had to remain at Tuskegee.

B<small>Y THE TIME</small> he turned 50, Booker T. Washington had been accused for years of being too friendly with white politicians, especially President Theodore Roosevelt, who had been reelected to office in the fall of 1904. As far as Washington's opponents were concerned, the educator was working hand in hand with Roosevelt, who was doing little to protect the civil rights of black Americans. Washington, of course, found himself in the awkward position of being the president's most intimate black adviser. It would not have been convenient, or expedient, for him to criticize Roosevelt's occasionally racist policies.

Two events in 1906 sorely tested Washington's faith in the current administration. On the night of August 13, a spray of gunfire caught the attention of everyone in the Mexican-border town of Brownsville, Texas. One white man was killed; another, a police official, was wounded. No one knew who had fired the shots, but the finger of guilt was pointed at the large regiment of black soldiers stationed at nearby Fort Brown.

A federal investigation was launched, but nothing could be proved one way or the other. The white citizens of Brownsville insisted the black soldiers had "shot up the town," and the soldiers denied it. At last, in October, the matter came to Roosevelt's direct attention. Washington begged the president to delay any action until he, Washington, could bring forth additional evidence regarding the case. Roosevelt's reply was impatient: "You can not have any information to give me privately to which I could pay heed, my dear Mr. Washington, because the information on which I act is that which came out in the investigation itself."

Shortly thereafter, Roosevelt instructed Secretary of War William Howard Taft to dishonorably discharge 167 men of the 25th Infantry Regiment. This was a blatantly discriminatory action, and millions of black Americans were outraged. "Of course," Washington wrote to a friend, "I am at a disadvantage in that I must keep my lips closed. The enemy will, as usual, try to blame me for all of this. They can talk; I cannot, without being disloyal to [Roosevelt], who I mean to stand by throughout his administration."

One month after the Brownsville shootings, the city of Atlanta, Georgia, witnessed a bloody race riot. On September 22, hundreds of angry white men armed themselves with guns, clubs, and chains and, without warning, descended upon Atlanta's black community. The mayor and police commissioner tried unsuccessfully to reason with the mob. The rampage lasted 5 days, and when it was over, 10 blacks and 1 white had been killed. To the dismay of southern blacks, Roosevelt claimed that he did not have the authority to send federal troops to suppress the mob violence.

Washington was in New York City during the Atlanta riot. He immediately sent a letter to the *New York World*, urging "the best white people and the best colored people to come together in council and use their united efforts to stop the present disorder." Additionally, he begged the black citizens of Atlanta "to exercise self-control and not make the fatal mistake of attempting to retaliate." Washington's critics considered this a mealymouthed response. Even the educator's friends were skeptical of such a passive approach. "I cannot believe," wrote T. Thomas Fortune, "that the policy of non-resistance in a situation like [this] can result in anything but contempt and massacre of the race."

Like all black Americans, Du Bois was deeply disturbed by the Brownsville incident and the Atlanta riot. For years, he had insisted that the Great Accommodator was "leading the way backward," and now a growing number of blacks began to think that maybe Du Bois was right, that Washington's policy of accommodation was fundamentally flawed. Moderation could not effectively combat the forces of racism in America; nor, apparently, could it bring the two races together in a meaningful way.

During the presidential campaign of 1908, Washington and his lieutenants worked vigorously on behalf of the Republican candidate, William Howard Taft. Buying the editorial support of black newspapers was only one of the many ways in which the Tuskegee Machine tried to convince black Americans that Taft was a better presidential choice than Democrat William Jennings Bryan, whose statements concerning blacks sounded distinctly hostile. Du Bois, meanwhile, reluctantly supported Bryan and urged others to do the same. "Use your ballots to defeat . . . the present dictatorship," he said. "Better vote for avowed enemies than for false friends."

Three months before the election, in August 1908, the attention of the nation was once again seized by a race riot, this one occurring in Springfield, Illinois, the hometown of Abraham Lincoln. Among those who witnessed the violence was a journalist named William English Walling, who wrote an

"The best friend that the Southern Negro can have is the Southern white man," said William Howard Taft, who succeeded Theodore Roosevelt as president and helped destroy the Tuskegee Machine that Washington had been building for more than a quarter of a century.

impassioned article about the riot for a northern periodical, the *Independent*. At the same time, he urged a "large and powerful body of citizens" to come to the aid of black Americans. "We must come to treat the Negro on a plane of absolute political and social equality," Walling wrote, a daring statement for a southern-bred white gentleman to make in 1908.

A number of northern whites were moved by Walling's article, including New York social workers Mary Ovington and Henry Moskovitz. A few months later, in January 1909, Ovington, Moskovitz, and Walling met in Manhattan to discuss what might be done to help the blacks. They decided that a large race conference should be held "for the discussion of present evils, the voicing of protests, and the renewal of the struggle for civil and political liberty."

An air of gloom must have hung over the small meeting. The state of Georgia had just adopted disfranchisement, and William Howard Taft was about to enter the Oval Office. In one of his speeches, the president-elect had made it clear that the federal government wanted "nothing to do with [the question of] social equality." Taft had also stated, with no trace of irony, that "the best friend that the Southern Negro can have is the Southern white man." Taft's apparent unwillingness to help black Americans convinced Walling and his friends that it was imperative to bring together all "believers in democracy" to fight the ugliness of race prejudice.

Among those who supported Walling's plan for a national race conference was Oswald Garrison Villard, the dynamic publisher of the *New York Evening Post*. In February, Villard printed a statement in his newspaper calling for such a conference to be held in New York City at the end of May. The statement was issued, symbolically, on February 12, the 100th anniversary of Abraham Lincoln's birth. It was signed by 60 prominent Americans, including social worker

Jane Addams, journalist Ida B. Wells-Barnett, philanthropist J. G. Phelps Stokes, and Du Bois. Realizing that their aims were nearly identical to those of the ailing Niagara Movement, the organizers of the conference encouraged Du Bois and his supporters to attend.

As the date for the conference approached, there was argument over whether Booker T. Washington should be invited. Villard had long admired Washington's work at Tuskegee, and five days before the conference, he took it upon himself to write a letter to the educator, carefully explaining the nature of the new organization. "It is not to be a Washington movement, or a Du Bois movement," Villard wrote. "The idea is that there shall grow out of it, first, an annual conference . . . [to discuss] the conditions of the colored people, politically, socially, industrially and educationally." The tone of Villard's letter was cautiously respectful. The organizers of the conference, he stated, "do not wish to embarrass you; they do not wish to seem to ignore you, or to leave you out. . . . On the other hand, they do not wish to tie you up with what may prove to be a radical political movement."

After giving it some thought, Washington decided not to attend. As he explained to Villard, he feared that his presence would inhibit discussion and possibly steer the organization in a direction that would be detrimental to its long-range goals. Nor did Washington have any desire to participate when he learned that several members of the Niagara Movement would be there. Instead, he sent one of his spies, Charles Anderson, to report on the three-day conference, which opened at the Henry Street Settlement in New York City on May 30, 1909.

The meeting was a mixed success. Many of the black participants, including William Monroe Trotter, were suspicious of their white colleagues, and by

Oswald Garrison Villard, publisher of the New York Evening Post *and grandson of noted abolitionist William Lloyd Garrison, was one of the founders of the National Association for the Advancement of Colored People (NAACP). Villard was also a great admirer of Washington's and invited him to take part in the 1909 conference that gave birth to the NAACP—an offer that Washington chose to decline.*

the final day of the conference, the atmosphere was unusually tense. Nevertheless, some good was accomplished. The group decided to name itself the National Negro Committee (NNC), and before the conference ended, on June 1, 40 people were appointed to carry out the NNC's work. Over the next few months, four additional conferences were held, during the course of which the NNC and the Niagara Movement formally merged. The second annual meeting of the NNC was held in May 1910, at which time the members agreed to adopt a new name: the National Association for the Advancement of Colored People (NAACP).

A handful of officers were duly elected. Moorfield Storey, a respected Boston lawyer, became the first president of the NAACP. Du Bois, the only black among the executive officers, was appointed director of publicity and research. Soon after, he moved to New York, where he launched the *Crisis*, the official publication of the NAACP. Under Du Bois's editorship, the *Crisis* became a powerful record of black protest and racial progress as well as a pointed weapon to use against Washington and the Tuskegee Machine.

From the beginning, Villard had hoped that Washington and Du Bois would be able to put aside

Despite its continued growth, Tuskegee Institute caused Washington constant worry because it required him to meet heavy financial obligations. "Perhaps," he said, "no one who has not gone through the experience, month after month, of trying to erect buildings and provide equipment for a school when no one knew where the money was to come from, can properly appreciate the difficulties under which we laboured."

their personal differences and work together to make the NAACP a potent force in American race relations. Washington, however, was deeply suspicious of the new organization. Its members, he claimed, were "bitter and resentful" people, frustrated intellectuals whose only aim was to discourage "the fundamentals of Hampton and Tuskegee and everything that we stand for." Repeatedly, he made it clear he wanted nothing to do with the NAACP or its militant policies.

In the summer of 1910, Washington sailed to Europe to do research for a book comparing the social and economic condition of black Americans with that of impoverished Europeans. Near the end of his three-month trip, he stopped in London, where he delivered a speech before the members of the Anti-Slavery and Aborigines Protection Society. As usual, he emphasized how well race relations were going in the United States, glossing over such embarrassments as lynching, segregation, and disfranchisement.

When Du Bois learned of Washington's speech, he wrote an open letter "To the People of Great Britain and Europe," attacking the educator for "giving the impression abroad that the Negro problem in America" was being satisfactorily solved. It was one thing, Du Bois declared, to be optimistic. It was quite another to deliberately "misrepresent the truth."

Du Bois's statement was signed by 32 prominent black Americans, many of them members of the NAACP. It was printed on NAACP letterhead, giving the impression that the executive committee of the NAACP supported Du Bois's attack (which it did not). Washington and his supporters were incensed by the letter, and though the incident was quickly forgotten by the public, it solidified Washington's antagonistic attitude toward the NAACP. With all that needed to be done concerning civil rights, he wrote to Villard, "it is difficult to see how people can throw away their time and strength in stirring up strife within the race."

Villard, naturally, was torn between his personal fondness for Washington and his deeper allegiance to the NAACP. Writing to Washington, he apologized for what had happened, claiming that Du Bois's letter "was absolutely accidental as far as this office was concerned." Then, gently, he reminded the educator that his optimism was leading him astray and, as a result, his popularity was slipping: "[A] greater and greater percentage of the intellectual colored people are turning from you and becoming your opponents, and with them a number of white people as well." Though it pained Washington to admit it, he knew that Villard was speaking the truth.

For the rest of his life, Washington publicly continued to stress the importance of accommodation, education, and economic advancement within the black community. But, increasingly, his message was falling upon deaf ears. Black Americans who had

Although Washington made every major decision at Tuskegee, he gave the institute's executive council the authority to run the school's daily affairs when he was away on business. The council consisted of his brother John (front row, right), treasurer Warren Logan (front row, second from right), private secretary Emmett Scott (front row, second from left), dean of women Jane Clark (front row, left), and the school's department heads, which included George Washington Carver (back row, right).

Washington relaxes in Jacksonville, Florida, in 1912. In the twilight of his career as a black leader, he saw his power dwindle as more and more people rejected his accommodationist policies.

once praised *Up from Slavery* for its homespun wisdom were now subscribing to the *Crisis* for its potent essays attacking racial injustice.

The formation and early success of the NAACP should not have surprised Washington. The Brownsville incident, the Atlanta and Springfield riots, and the subtle racism of the Republican party had all underscored the need in America for a strong civil rights organization. Washington, however, refused to heed the signs. In his personal vendetta against Du Bois and the NAACP, he failed to realize that history was passing him by. ❧

13

A NEW FRANKNESS

ON THE EVENING of Sunday, March 19, 1911, Booker T. Washington was in New York City, where earlier that day he had given two public speeches. After a light supper, he took the subway uptown to the West Side, departing near the southern end of Central Park. From there he walked to an apartment building on West 63rd Street, a few blocks from the Tenderloin, one of New York's seediest neighborhoods. As Washington later explained to the press, he had come to this questionable part of town to visit Daniel C. Smith, the auditor for Tuskegee Institute.

Around nine o'clock in the evening, Washington entered the lobby of the building where he had been told Smith was staying with friends. After checking the directory, he rang the bell and waited. No answer. At this moment, an attractive young woman passed him, heading for the street. A minute or so later, Washington also went outside, where he paced up and down the sidewalk, waiting for Smith to return. The same woman passed him again. She would later claim that Washington had spoken to her in a forward

---

In the last years of his life, Washington publicly kept up his grueling pace as an educator and leader of his race. He began, however, to speak out against racism more forcefully than ever before.

manner: "He looked me right in the face and said, 'Hello, sweetheart.'"

After a while, Washington returned to the lobby, pressed the bell, and waited. Still no answer. He went outside again, walked a bit, returned again, and rang the bell. His behavior must have looked suspicious to anyone observing him. According to Washington, he had just put on his glasses and was peering at the directory when a white man, Henry Ulrich, burst in from the street. "What are you doing here?" Ulrich demanded. "Are you breaking into my house? You have been hanging around here for four or five weeks!" Without waiting for an answer, Ulrich began to hit Washington on the head with his fist. Washington tried to explain, but the man was infuriated.

At last, bruised and battered, Washington fled through the outside door and ran down the sidewalk, his assailant following close behind. Seizing a cane from a passerby, Ulrich began to rain blows upon Washington's head. After running a block, Washington tripped and fell, landing almost at the feet of a policeman. Blood was streaming from his head and mouth. "This man is a thief," Ulrich told the police officer. "I found him with his hand on the door-knob and his eye at the keyhole."

Washington was arrested and taken to a nearby station house. There, with difficulty, he managed to explain who he was and what had happened. All charges against him were immediately dismissed. Washington was then taken to the hospital, where his wounds were treated. He might have let the matter drop, but instead he charged Ulrich with felonious assault (later reduced to simple assault). A trial date was set for the following November.

During his convalescence, Washington received dozens of comforting letters and telegrams, including messages from Theodore Roosevelt and President William Howard Taft. In a halfhearted show of support, the NAACP passed a resolution expressing "profound regret" at this "renewed evidence of racial discrimination." Even William Monroe Trotter resisted the urge to gloat over his rival's misfortune. "Our opposition to Mr. Washington . . . is well known," he wrote in the *Boston Guardian*, "but we do not desire to take any advantage of his present troubles. We want to fight men when [they are] standing up."

As long as Washington's head was swathed in bandages, the public was sympathetic. By the time the Ulrich case came to court, however, all sorts of rumors had begun to spread. It was whispered that Washington had been drinking that night; that it was he who had started the fight; that he had come to that "free and easy" neighborhood seeking the companionship of white women. Unfortunately, Washington was not able to satisfactorily explain his presence at the apartment building. Repeatedly, he insisted that he had gone there to meet Daniel Smith, Tuskegee's auditor—but Smith lived in New Jersey, not New York, and in any event Smith was at Tuskegee on the night of the beating.

At the trial, which was held on November 6, Washington and Ulrich stuck by their respective stories. It seemed obvious to most people in the courtroom that Ulrich was stretching the truth, but it seemed equally obvious that Washington was being evasive. After evidence had been presented from both sides, Ulrich was acquitted of the charge of assaulting Washington. According to the *New York Age*, the audience in the courtroom was "astounded" by the judges' decision.

To this day, the Ulrich affair continues to mystify Washington's biographers. What was he doing in that particular neighborhood on the night of March 19? The answer may never be known. As far as Washington's career was concerned, the sensational publicity

On March 19, 1911, a white assailant beat Washington with a walking stick outside a New York City apartment building. The black leader's opponents seized this opportunity to cast a cloud of doubt over his integrity through political cartoons and other means.

surrounding the Ulrich case did no lasting damage. Washington's friends continued to support him, and those who disliked him felt justified in their antipathy. Nevertheless, it was a strange and troubling incident, one that left an unfortunate blemish on Washington's otherwise spotless reputation.

By the time the Ulrich trial came to an end, the 1912 presidential campaign was getting under way. Most black Americans were fearful that Taft might be reelected. In the opinion of some, his administration had marked a low point in the history of American race relations. Even before his inauguration, Taft had begun the discriminatory process of removing nearly all black men from southern political office.

His first victim was William Crum, collector of customs in Charleston, the black man for whose confirmation Theodore Roosevelt had battled Congress for two years. After Crum, southern black officeholders began to fall like ninepins. The few black men who continued to work for the government held unimportant, low-visibility positions. On at least two occasions, Taft implied to Washington that he had a long-range plan that would please blacks; if this is true, it was never revealed to the public. Taft's strategy was to put off for as long as possible the disagreeable task of dealing with what was commonly called "the negro problem."

In the presidential campaign of 1912, Taft ran on the Republican ticket. Former president Roosevelt, hoping to win a third term, quickly formed the Progressive party, which had no room on its "progressive" platform for black civil rights. Unwittingly, Taft and Roosevelt split the Republican vote, giving the presidential victory to a Democrat, Woodrow Wilson, who, during his campaign, had promised to treat blacks with "absolute fair dealing." Less than three weeks after Wilson took office, however, Washington was already expressing private concern about the president's sincerity: "I fear [his] high-sounding phrases regarding justice do not include the Negro."

Washington was right: Wilson had no intention of improving the political or social status of black Americans during his administration. He continued Taft's strategy of removing blacks from federal office, and to his chagrin, Washington found he was no longer being consulted on matters relating to race. In the eyes of the Democratic party, the Great Accommodator was a nuisance and—after the Ulrich affair—a potential liability. Through lack of use, the gears of the Tuskegee Machine began to grow rusty.

Shortly after Wilson's inauguration, a strict policy of segregation was adopted by many branches of the federal government, including the U.S. Postal Service, which had traditionally been a safe haven for blacks. Trotter, for one, was outraged by the new policy, and in November 1914, he led a delegation of blacks to the White House to accuse Wilson of breaking his campaign promises and to force him "to square his actions with his words." The meeting did not go well, with the conversation descending into a heated series of accusations and denials.

The issue of segregation was one that had troubled Washington since the beginning of his public career. In November 1912—the month Wilson was elected president—Washington wrote a bold article entitled "Is the Negro Having a Fair Chance?" After examining the question from various angles, he concluded that black Americans had little reason to be satisfied, especially in the area of railway transportation. "What embitters the colored people in regard to railroad travel," he wrote, "is not the separation but the inadequacy of the accommodations. . . . In most cases, the Negro portion of the car is poorly ventilated, poorly lighted, and, above all, rarely kept clean." In addition to the miseries of railroad travel,

"I fear the President's high-sounding phrases regarding justice do not include the Negro," Washington said in 1913 of Woodrow Wilson, who succeeded William Howard Taft in the White House. Wilson's refusal to improve the political or social status of black Americans prompted Washington to become more outspoken on civil rights issues.

Washington stands in his vegetable garden at Tuskegee. "I think I owe a great deal of my present strength and ability to work to my love of out-door life," he wrote in My Larger Education. "It is true that the amount of time that I can spend in the open air is now very limited. Taken on an average, it is not more than an hour a day, but I make the most of that hour."

Washington explored such issues as lynching, disfranchisement, and the inadequacies of black education.

The article, which appeared in *Century* magazine, was later printed in pamphlet form and distributed to railroad officials throughout the South. Its frank tone took many people by surprise, including W. E. B. Du Bois, who noted with pleasure "that Mr. Booker T. Washington has joined the ranks." Though Du Bois was overstating the case, it is true that after Woodrow Wilson was elected to office, Washington began to speak out against racism more forcefully than he had ever done before. He was certainly no rabble-rouser, but in a variety of ways he did make his feelings known.

On one occasion, in Tampa, Florida, Washington was scheduled to address a large crowd. As soon as he entered the theater, he saw a line of bed sheets hanging down the middle of the aisle. Washington was clearly annoyed. "I have traveled all over this country and in many foreign lands," he said firmly, "but this is the first time that I have ever seen white people and colored people separated by sheets. Now, before I begin my remarks, I want that thing taken down from there." The sheets were removed.

Unfortunately, Washington's attempts to expose the ugliness of racism were not strong enough or frequent enough to have much impact. An accommodationist at heart, he could never attack the system of white supremacy with any real vigor. For too many years, his public statements concerning lynching and other injustices had been frustratingly ambiguous, and to a large degree this had undermined his effectiveness as a racial spokesman. By 1913, a large number of blacks had turned against him, and as the NAACP continued to grow in size and prestige, the Tuskegee educator seemed to many an embarrassing relic from the past. Even Oswald Garrison Villard, who liked Washington, was forced to admit privately that his friend's name "is getting to be anathema among the educated colored people in the country, and he is drifting further and further in the rear as a real leader."

Though Washington's influence was declining, his level of activity was not. During the last years of his life, he was as busy as ever running his school, overseeing the Tuskegee Negro Conference, keeping his eye on Du Bois and the NAACP, raising much-needed funds, and giving speeches throughout the country. With the help of various collaborators and ghostwriters, he turned out numerous books, including *The Story of the Negro* (1909) and *My Larger Education* (1911). He also wrote a biography of Frederick Douglass (1907) as well as a book about his European travels and observations, *The Man Farthest Down* (1912). None of these volumes duplicated the success of *Up from Slavery*, but they were widely read and helped maintain Washington's position as the most famous black man in the world.

In addition to his work with the National Negro Business League, Washington began to give speeches on behalf of a new organization, the National Urban League (NUL). Founded in 1910, the NUL addressed the various problems faced by southern blacks who were moving in increasing numbers to the northern cities, where they hoped to find better living conditions and greater economic opportunities. Because he regarded the NUL's approach as constructive, Washington was able to give it his enthusiastic support, something he could never do for the NAACP.

It was his ongoing work at Tuskegee, however, that gave Washington his deepest satisfaction. In his 34-year career as principal, he never lost interest in the growth and progress of his school. Many mornings, he would don a pair of overalls and stroll around the campus, jotting down his observations in a notebook. He watched the cows and horses being fed; he himself went to the henhouse and collected the eggs. He loved his vegetable garden and swore that Tuskegee eggs and fresh-grown Tuskegee carrots were superior to anything he could order in a restaurant. He spent as much time as he could around the pigpen. "The pig, I think, is my favorite animal," he once wrote. "I do not know how this will strike the taste of my readers, but it is true . . . and it is a real pleasure to me to watch their development and increase from month to month."

In April 1914, Washington celebrated his 58th birthday. His health was beginning to fail, and, appropriately, it was during this period that he turned his attention to the neglected subject of health care for black Americans. That year, he broadened the scope of the Tuskegee Negro Conference to include a separate health conference, which was attended by thousands of people. Among the issues discussed were water impurity, the dangers of alcohol, fraudulent medicines, tuberculosis among blacks, and—a Washington touch—the importance of daily bathing. Speaking to the crowd, he encouraged whites to take

From March 21 to 27, 1915, Washington (front row, fifth from left) and his aides sponsored National Negro Health Week, an intensive effort to improve the sanitary and health conditions of blacks. By then, Washington's own health had begun to fail.

greater interest in the subject of quality health care for blacks. "The life of the humblest black person in the South," he said, "in some way touches the life of the most exalted white person in the South." The following year, Washington founded National Negro Health Week, March 21–27, 1915.

During the last year of his life, as World War I was being fought in Europe, Washington single-handedly orchestrated a letter-writing campaign against a wartime bill that would prevent any European or dark-skinned person from immigrating to the United States after the war. Though the bill had already been passed in the Senate, it was defeated in the House of Representatives, 250 to 77. The success of Washington's letter-writing campaign raised the racial hopes of at least one black newspaper, the *Chicago Defender*: "Wouldn't it be a glorious thing if the Booker T. Washington faction, the Du Bois faction, and the Monroe Trotter faction would get together on a common ground and fight unitedly for the things that they are now fighting singly for?"

Common ground presented itself sooner than anyone expected. During the last months of Washington's life, he, Trotter, and the NAACP joined forces to denounce D. W. Griffith's *The Birth of a*

Nation, a brilliant but corrosive film that, among other things, glorified the white supremacist group the Ku Klux Klan. Despite vigorous protests, Washington and his colleagues were unsuccessful in their attempt to ban *The Birth of a Nation*, which at that time was the longest and most elaborate motion picture ever made. That fall, there was talk of turning *Up from Slavery* into a film, but Washington's death put an end to all negotiations.

It has been said, with some validity, that Washington killed himself through overwork. Every day, whether he was at Tuskegee or on the road, he dealt with a tremendous amount of personal and professional paperwork. Businessmen asked for his advice; politicians asked for his endorsement; philanthropists wrote, requesting detailed reports about how their money was being spent. Schools and other institutions were eager to know how they, too, could tap into Andrew Carnegie's wealth.

Washington was flooded with speaking requests, invitations, bills, with every sort of correspondence imaginable. Could he recommend a suitable person for such and such a position? Could he make a speech to the Negro Women's Club? To the Loyal Temperance Union? To the state convict board? Could he give an interview to a northern journalist? Would he be interested in contributing money toward the establishment of an all-black town? The requests never stopped coming, and Washington never stopped working. In retrospect, it seems incredible that he was able to maintain his pace for as long as he did.

Early in November 1915, his health finally broke. He was in New York City, raising funds for Tuskegee Institute and making a number of public speeches. On November 4, he planned to travel by train to Petersburg, Virginia, to make a speech before a black organization. Before he could depart, however, he became ill, and his New York doctors convinced him to enter St. Luke's Hospital for observation. Washington must have sensed that something was seriously wrong. On November 5, he sent a telegram to his wife at Tuskegee, telling her to "come at once."

A handful of people knew that Washington was suffering from kidney trouble and that his blood pressure was extremely high. He was also prone to attacks of indigestion. The exact nature of his illness, however, remains unclear. Emmett Scott later wrote that during the last weeks of Washington's life he was "wasted by disease and suffering almost constant pain."

From his hospital bed at St. Luke's, Washington continued to conduct business, firing off numerous telegrams to his staff at Tuskegee. For nearly a week, his condition was a closely guarded secret, but on November 10 the story hit the papers. Washington was reported to be suffering the effects of a nervous breakdown. His doctor told the press that his patient was "ageing rapidly" and "extremely nervous." A rumor began to spread that Washington was dying from syphilis. The trustees at Tuskegee, meanwhile, admitted they had no one in mind to replace Washington as principal.

Despite the care of several physicians, Washington grew weaker every day. At last, realizing the gravity of his condition, he insisted on returning to Tuskegee. "I was born in the South," he said, "I have lived and labored in the South, and I expect to die and be buried in the South."

He and his wife Maggie took the train for Tuskegee on the afternoon of November 12. Washington arrived, barely alive, at approximately nine o'clock that evening. On the way to the institute, he apparently lost consciousness. A few hours later, in the presence of his family, he died at 4:45 A.M., Sunday, November 13, 1915. Shortly thereafter, the

"I do not overlook the wrongs that often perplex and embarrass us in this country," Washington said in 1911. "…I condemn any practice in any state that results in not enforcing the law with a certainty and justice, regardless of race or color."

Washington's body is buried in a little cemetery on the Tuskegee Institute campus on November 16, 1915, three days after his death.

bells began to peal on campus, calling the students to begin their day.

Gradually, the news spread that Washington had died. Everyone was stunned. According to the *Montgomery Advertiser*, there was throughout the city of Tuskegee a "feeling of personal loss. Nobody is hiding his tears. Nobody is free from gloom." The most powerful and most respected black man in the United States was dead. One poet, Claude McKay, tenderly expressed the sorrow felt by millions: "Death's hand has torn you from your trusting race, / And O! we feel so utterly alone."

In the December issue of the *Crisis*, Du Bois attempted to put Washington's life into perspective. "He was the greatest Negro leader since Frederick Douglass," Du Bois wrote. "On the other hand, in stern justice, we must lay on the soul of this man, a heavy responsibility for the consummation of Negro disfranchisement, the decline of the Negro college and public school and the firmer establishment of color caste."

There was some truth to what Du Bois said, and, historically, this is the image of Washington that has been perpetuated to the present day. To assess Washington properly, however, he must be viewed in the context of his time. It is unlikely that he or any other black leader could have ended the myriad forms of racism that characterized the post–Civil War period. As one of Washington's biographers has observed, Washington "accepted half a loaf, not as a permanent settlement, but as a means toward obtaining the whole loaf later. To criticize his methods is to make the facile assumption that he had some choice in the matter. He did what was possible, given the time and place in which he lived, and did it to the utmost."

Though Washington advocated a policy of black submission, he did not lead the way backward, as Du Bois so often claimed. Nor did he hate the NAACP, as many people assume. Washington may not have approved of the NAACP's methods or personalities, but he never questioned for a moment its ultimate goal: that of obtaining equal justice under the law for every black American.

"More and more," he said, "we must learn to think not in terms of race or color or language or religion or political boundaries, but in terms of humanity." Seen in this light, Washington's message of brotherhood continues to be relevant today. Each time two races, or two nations, attempt to forge a bond of peace and understanding, the spirit of Booker T. Washington lives on. ❧

CHRONOLOGY

—— ❦ ——

1856   Born on April 5 near Hale's Ford, Virginia

1865   Moves with family to Malden, West Virginia

1872   Enrolls at Hampton Normal and Agricultural Institute in Hampton, Virginia

1875   Graduates from Hampton Institute; begins teaching at black school in Tinkersville, West Virginia

1878   Attends Wayland Seminary in Washington, D.C.

1879   Returns to Hampton Institute as faculty member

1881   Opens Tuskegee Normal and Industrial Institute in Tuskegee, Alabama

1882   Marries first wife, Fanny Smith

1883   Daughter, Portia, is born

1884   Fanny Washington dies

1885   BTW marries second wife, Olivia Davidson; son, Booker T., Jr., is born

1889   Son, Ernest Davidson, is born; Olivia Washington dies

1892   First Tuskegee Negro Conference is held; BTW marries third wife, Margaret Murray

1895   Delivers Atlanta Compromise speech at the Cotton States and International Exposition in Atlanta, Georgia, on September 18

1899   Travels to Europe

1900   Founds National Negro Business League

1901   Publication of *Up from Slavery*; BTW dines at the White House on October 16

1903   Andrew Carnegie gives $600,000 to Tuskegee Institute; BTW travels to Europe

1904   Organizes a three-day conference of black leaders at New York City's Carnegie Hall; BTW adopts daughter, Laura Murray

1906   Celebrates 25th anniversary of Tuskegee Institute

1909   Refuses to attend conference that gives birth to the National Association for the Advancement of Colored People (NAACP)

1911   Publication of *My Larger Education*; BTW attacked by Henry Ulrich in New York City

1915   Sponsors National Negro Health Week; dies on November 13 in Tuskegee

FURTHER READING

Adair, Gene. *George Washington Carver*. New York: Chelsea House, 1989.

Butler, B. N. "Booker T. Washington, W. E. B. Du Bois, Black Americans and the NAACP." *Crisis* 85 (August 1978): 222–30.

Du Bois, W. E. B. *The Souls of Black Folk: Essays and Sketches*. 1903. Reprint. New York: Vintage Books/Library of America, 1990.

Fox, Stephen R. *The Guardian of Boston: William Monroe Trotter*. New York: Atheneum, 1970.

Harlan, Louis R. *Booker T. Washington: The Making of a Black Leader, 1856–1901*. New York: Oxford University Press, 1972.

———. *Booker T. Washington: The Wizard of Tuskegee, 1901–1915*. New York: Oxford University Press, 1983.

Mathews, Basil. *Booker T. Washington: Educator and Interracial Interpreter*. Cambridge: Harvard University Press, 1948.

Meier, August. *Negro Thought in America, 1880–1915: Racial Ideologies in the Age of Booker T. Washington*. Ann Arbor: University of Michigan Press, 1963.

Scott, Emmett J. and Lyman B. Stowe. *Booker T. Washington: Builder of a Civilization*. Garden City, NY: Doubleday, 1916.

Spencer, Jr., Samuel R. *Booker T. Washington and the Negro's Place in American Life*. Boston: Little, Brown, 1955.

Stafford, Mark. *W. E. B. Du Bois*. New York: Chelsea House, 1989

Washington, Booker T. *My Larger Education*. Garden City, NY: Doubleday, 1911.

———. *Up from Slavery*. 1901. Reprint. New York: Viking Penguin, 1986.

Washington, E. Davidson, ed. *Selected Speeches of Booker T. Washington*. Garden City, NY: Doubleday, 1932.

INDEX

ALAN SCHROEDER is the author of two other biographies published by Chelsea House, *Josephine Baker* and *Jack London*. He is also the author of *Ragtime Tumpie*, an acclaimed account of Josephine Baker's childhood in St. Louis. Selected as one of the Best Books of the Year by *Parents* magazine and the *Boston Globe*, *Ragtime Tumpie* was also named a Notable Children's Book of 1989 by the American Library Association. Mr. Schroeder lives in Alameda, California.

NATHAN IRVIN HUGGINS, one of America's leading scholars in the field of black studies, helped select the titles for the BLACK AMERICANS OF ACHIEVEMENT series, for which he also served as senior consulting editor. He was the W.E.B. Du Bois Professor of History and of Afro-American Studies at Harvard University and the director of the W.E.B. Du Bois Institute for Afro-American Research at Harvard. He received his doctorate from Harvard in 1962 and returned there as a professor in 1980 after teaching at Columbia University, the University of Massachusetts, Lake Forest College, and the California State University, Long Beach. He was the author of four books and dozens of articles, including *Black Odyssey: The Afro-American Ordeal in Slavery*, *The Harlem Renaissance*, and *Slave and Citizen: The Life of Frederick Douglass*, and was associated with the Children's Television Workshop, National Public Radio, the Boston Athenaeum, the Museum of Afro-American History, the Howard Thurman Educational Trust, and Upward Bound. Professor Huggins died in 1989, at the age of 62, in Cambridge, Massachusetts.

PICTURE CREDITS